Making Mascot Dolls

Making Mascot Dolls

Jean Greenhowe

B T Batsford Ltd London

ISBN 0 7134 2177 9

Typeset in IBM Century 9 on 11pt. by Tek-Art
Printed in Great Britain by
Butler & Tanner Ltd, Frome, Somerset
for the publishers, B.T.Batsford Ltd,
4 Fitzhardinge Street, London W1H 0AH

Contents

Introduction

This book contains full instructions and patterns for making 30 mascot dolls each about 30 cm (12 in) in height. In addition there are details for making another 30 dolls by simply using patterns given throughout the book.

The variety of dolls ranges from sporting mascots like the footballer, show jumper and skier, to dolls for special occasions such as the bride and groom and Santa Claus. There are dolls for Wild West enthusiasts and up-to-date dolls in the shape of the pop star, space hero and film star. Fictional and fun characters are also represented by Cinderella, Robin Hood, the pirate and the clown, to name but a few.

All the dolls are constructed in the same way from simple stuffed tubes of fabric which also form the basic garments. Only small amounts of fabrics and trimmings are required so that they are very economical to make. The patterns are printed full size for tracing directly off the pages and these provide endless possibilities for making many more characters as well as those described in the list of further suggestions.

I have particularly enjoyed creating the mascot dolls for this book and hope that some of my enthusiasm may be conveyed to the reader.

General instructions

Quantities of materials   The quantities of materials and trimmings required are not given with each mascot since the pieces are so small that they can probably be found in the household rag bag, or among toymaking cuttings. If, however, it should be necessary to purchase materials, the amounts can be calculated by taking a note of the measurements in the instructions or by refering to the sizes of the pattern pieces. A list, suggesting the most suitable materials to use, is provided with each mascot, plus details of any additional items which may be required for accessories.

Cotton stockinette   This is used for making the dolls' heads and hands and it can be white or tinted with cold water dye. Pink stockinette can be obtained from the address in the suppliers' list. Alternatively, cuttings off old plain white T-shirts can be used.

Cut out the stockinette pieces having the most stretch in the fabric (usually across the width) in the direction shown on the pattern pieces.

Knitting yarn   Chunky or double knitting yarn is required for the dolls' hair in most cases. One ball is sufficient for several dolls. Use suitable shades of brown, yellow, tan or black.

Strong thread   This is used for stab stitching through the centre of each doll's body to form the legs and it should match the fabric. Button thread is ideal but it is usually only obtainable in black, white, grey or brown. However, white thread can be coloured with marker pen to match the body fabric after the stitching is completed.

Stuffing   Either kapok or man-made fibre filling is suitable. Foam chips should not be used as they are too lumpy.

Red pencil This is used for colouring the dolls' cheeks and noses. It should be rubbed gently onto the fabric.

Cardboard Cardboard is needed for the base of each doll. Discarded household packages such as breakfast cereal and detergent boxes provide a useful supply. Two or three layers should be glued together to make the base rigid and firm.

Felt This is required for making some of the items of clothing and also for the dolls' eyes.

Leather cloth Occasionally this is used for the dolls' feet or belts but felt can be used instead.

Fur fabric This is sometimes used for the dolls' hair instead of yarn and also for items of clothing. Always cut out the pieces so that the smooth stroke of the fur pile is in the direction indicated on the pattern pieces. When cutting out fur fabric pieces, snip through the back of the fabric only so as not to cut through the fur pile.

Seams and turnings 1 cm ($\frac{3}{8}$ in) seams and turnings are allowed on all pieces unless other details are given. Join all fabrics with the right sides together unless otherwise stated.

Patterns All patterns are given actual size for tracing directly off the pages. Some pattern edges are marked 'place this edge to fold in fabric'; in this case pin the pattern to folded fabric and cut out through double thickness to obtain the full-sized piece.

Glueing When adhesive is mentioned in the instructions it should be a quick-drying general purpose type, such as UHU or Elmer's Glue-All. Unwanted smears of this adhesive can be removed by dabbing with a cloth dipped in a little acetone. Take care when using acetone as it is highly inflammable.

Before cutting out very small felt shapes, such as the dolls' eyes, first spread the back of the felt with adhesive and allow it to dry. This will ensure that the cut-out shape has clean, smooth edges.

Tools No special tools are required for making the dolls except for those used in ordinary sewing, plus a ruler. A pair of compasses will be found useful for drawing out the occasional circular pattern, as well as tweezers for positioning small pieces such as the dolls' eyes.

Metric and imperial measurements The sizes given throughout this book have been worked out individually both in metric and imperial so that in many instances the measurements are not absolutely accurate conversions of each other. This is to avoid having awkward sizes when a little extra either way will make no difference to the appearance of the finished doll. The reader should use either one or the other throughout for each mascot.

The safety factor in toys for children Although it is unlikely that a mascot-type doll would be made for a very young child, it is worth mentioning here that such children should not be given dolls or toys containing wire, beads, buttons, or any other items which could be dangerous or could become detached and swallowed.

Constructing the basic doll

The patterns   Firstly, trace all the basic doll patterns off the pages. Note that the upper and lower body pieces need to be traced onto folded paper, placing the folds in the paper to the dotted lines indicated on the patterns. Cut out the patterns and open up the folded upper and lower body pieces to give the full-sized patterns.

To make the body   Cut out the upper and lower body pieces using suitable materials as set out in the instructions for each doll. Run a contrasting coloured tacking thread up the centre front of the lower body piece as shown on the pattern. Run a gathering thread along the waist edge of the lower body piece and pull up the gathers slightly until this edge fits the waist edge of the upper body piece. Join the pieces at the waist edge as shown in diagram 1. Now join the centre back edges of the upper and lower body pieces. Turn the lower raw edge to the wrong side and tack in place as shown in diagram 2.

Cut the base from card, glueing two or three layers together if necessary to make the base fairly rigid. The base is next covered with felt and details are given with each doll as to whether this should match the fabric used for the pants, the legs or the feet. Glue the base to a piece of felt, then cut out the felt a little larger all round than the base. Glue the other side of the base to a piece of felt and cut out in

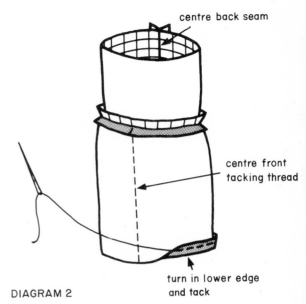

centre back seam

centre front tacking thread

turn in lower edge and tack

DIAGRAM 2

the same way. Now oversew the edges of the felt together all round the base as shown in diagram 3.

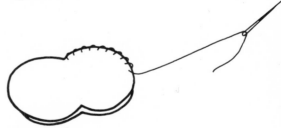

DIAGRAM 3
oversew the edges of the felt together all round the base

Slip the base inside the lower edge of the lower body piece matching the centre front and back points of base and body. Oversew the edge of the body to the edge of the base all round as shown in diagram 4. Now turn the body right side out. Stuff the body firmly, then turn in the neck edge and run round a strong gathering thread. Pull up the gathers slightly.

To make the neck   Cut the neck strip from white or pink felt. Roll up the strip tightly along the length and oversew the short edge in place. Slip half of the

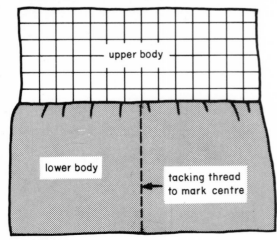

upper body

lower body

tacking thread to mark centre

DIAGRAM 1
joining the upper body to the lower body

8

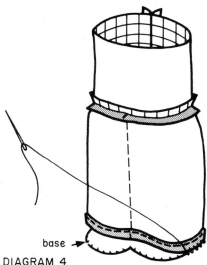

base →

DIAGRAM 4
oversew lower edge of body to base
matching centre front and back points

neck inside the gathered top edge of the body, pull
up the gathers tightly around the neck and fasten
off. Sew the body fabric to the neck all
round as shown in diagram 5.

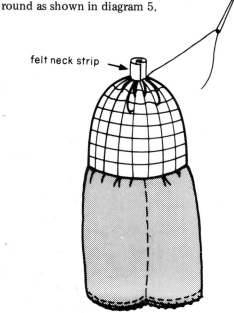

felt neck strip →

DIAGRAM 5 sewing the neck in place

To form the legs   Thread a darning needle with a
2 m (2yd) length of strong thread and knot the ends
of the thread together. Take the needle through the
doll's leg to the centre back, close to the base. Pull
the needle through but leave the knotted ends of the
thread protruding as shown in diagram 6. Now take
a couple of oversewing stitches in the fabric close to
the base to secure the thread. Snip off the knotted
thread ends.

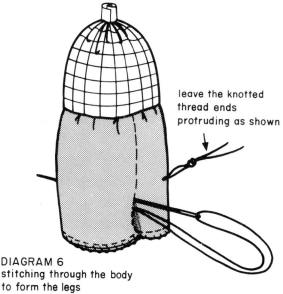

leave the knotted
thread ends
protruding as shown

DIAGRAM 6
stitching through the body
to form the legs

Now take the needle straight through the body
to the tacking thread at the front. Take a small
stitch above this, passing the needle through the
doll to the centre back seam again. Pull the thread
tightly. Continue in this way as shown in diagram
6, working up the body for about 8 cm (3¼ in) and
pulling the thread tightly all the time. Take the last
stitch through to the back of the doll.

To fasten off the thread, cut it to divide in two,
then take one thread through the doll and back again
and knot the threads tightly. Pass the threads through
to the side of the doll's legs as when starting and snip
off the ends. Remove the centre and lower edge
tacking threads.

To make the feet   For most of the dolls these are
made from felt and will form either the shoes or

9

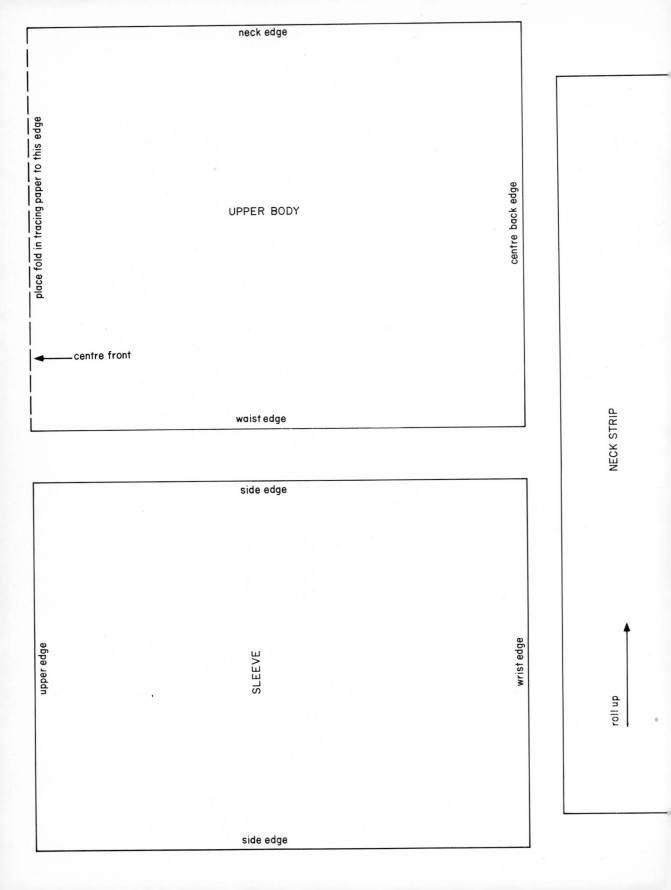

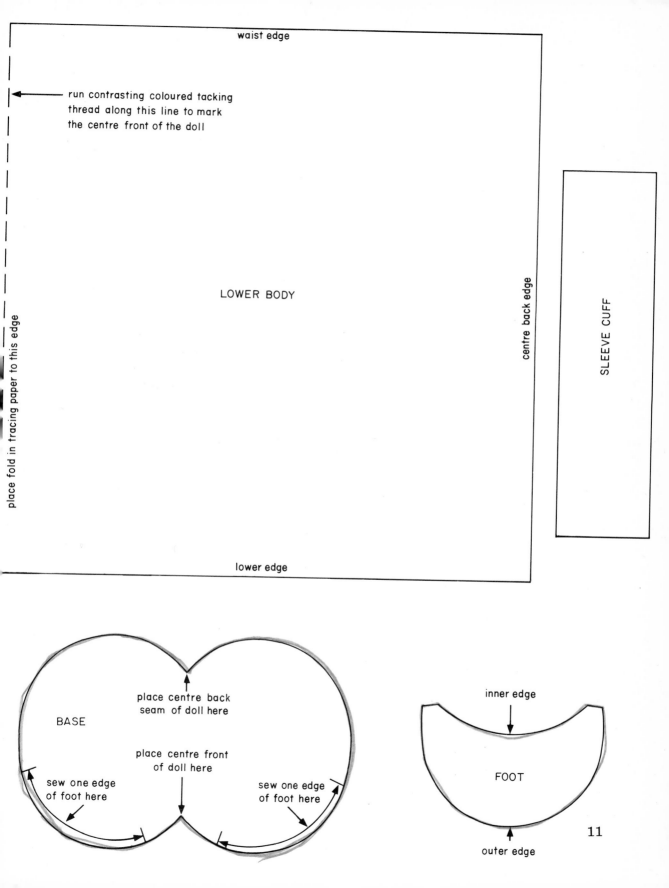

waist edge

run contrasting coloured tacking
thread along this line to mark
the centre front of the doll

place fold in tracing paper to this edge

LOWER BODY

centre back edge

SLEEVE CUFF

lower edge

BASE

place centre back
seam of doll here

place centre front
of doll here

sew one edge
of foot here

sew one edge
of foot here

inner edge

FOOT

outer edge

11

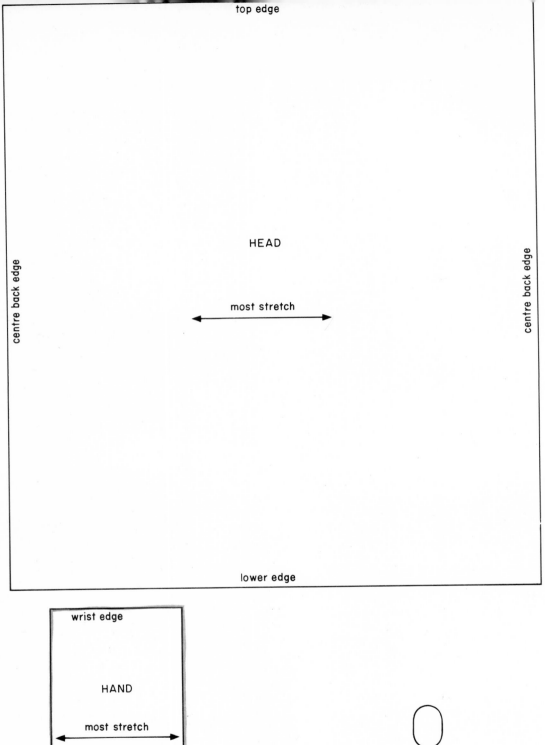

top edge

centre back edge

centre back edge

HEAD

most stretch

lower edge

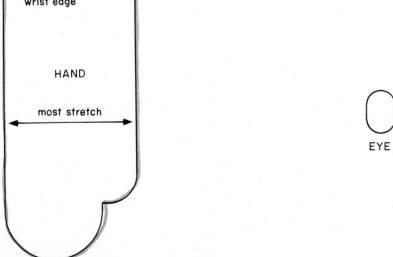

wrist edge

HAND

most stretch

EYE

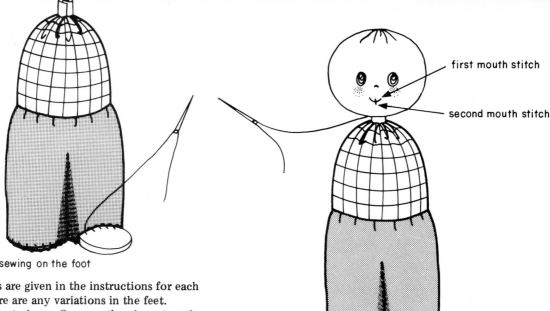

DIAGRAM 7 sewing on the foot

DIAGRAM 8 attaching the head

first mouth stitch

second mouth stitch

boots. Details are given in the instructions for each mascot if there are any variations in the feet.

Cut four foot pieces. Oversew the pieces together in pairs round the outer edges. Turn the feet right side out and push a little stuffing inside them. Place the feet in front of the doll and oversew one inner edge of each foot to the base at the positions shown on the base pattern. Slip stitch the remaining inner edges of the feet to the legs as shown in diagram 7.

On some of the girl dolls the legs will form the pantaloons. In these cases sew narrow lace edging all round the lower edge of the legs, taking it over the feet at the front.

To make the head   Cut the head from stockinette and join the centre back edges. Run a gathering thread round 1 cm ($\frac{3}{8}$ in) from the top edge, pull up the gathers tightly and fasten off. Turn the head right side out and stuff to measure about 25cm (9¾ in) around.

Run a gathering thread round 1 cm ($\frac{3}{8}$ in) away from the lower edge. Turn in the raw edge and pull up the gathers a little. Place this gathered edge over the neck then pull up the gathers tightly leaving about 5 mm (¼ in) of the neck exposed between the body and head as shown in diagram 8. Fasten off the thread and sew the head fabric to the neck all round.

To make the face   Any variations in facial features are given in the individual instructions for each mascot. For the basic face cut the eyes from black felt. Glue them in place half-way down the head and 2.5 cm (1 in) apart.

For the mouth use red thread and a long needle. Secure the end of the thread at the back of the head, then take it through the head to the face and make a

1 cm ($\frac{3}{8}$ in) long stitch 1.5 cm ($\frac{5}{8}$ in) below the eyes. Fasten off the thread at the back of the head. Take another tiny stitch in the same way, below and around the centre of the first stitch, to pull it into a U-shaped curve as shown in diagram 8.

Use the moistened tip of a red pencil to mark the nose between the eyes then colour the cheeks also by rubbing the fabric with the dry pencil.

To make the hands and sleeves   The hands are made from stockinette on most of the dolls unless other instructions are given. Cut two pairs of hand pieces and join them taking 3 mm ($\frac{1}{8}$ in) seams and leaving the wrist edges open. Trim the seams and turn the hands right side out. Stuff the hands, then run a gathering thread round each wrist edge. Pull up the gathers tightly and fasten off.

Cut the sleeves from fabric. Join the side edges then turn right side out. Turn in the wrist edge of each sleeve and slip it over the gathered end of the hand as shown in diagram 9. Slip stitch the sleeves to the hands as shown in diagram 10. Stuff the sleeves lightly then turn in the upper edges and slip stitch, turning in the corners to round off the tops of the sleeves as shown in diagram 10.

Sew the tops of the sleeves to each side of the body 2.5 cm (1 in) down from the neck as shown in diagram 11, having the thumbs pointing towards the body.

13

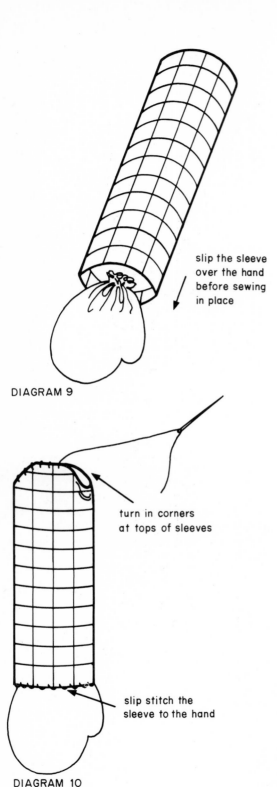

slip the sleeve
over the hand
before sewing
in place

DIAGRAM 9

turn in corners
at tops of sleeves

slip stitch the
sleeve to the hand

DIAGRAM 10

DIAGRAM 11

If the doll's sleeves have cuffs make these as follows. Cut the cuffs from fabric then turn in all the raw edges 5 mm (¼ in) and press. Place a cuff around each wrist then lap one short end over the other and sew in place.

To make the boy's basic hair style Most of the dolls have a head covering of some kind and for these only a fringe of hair is required.

Wind the strand of yarn straight off the ball, four times around two fingers. Slip these loops off the fingers and back stitch them to the doll's head about 3 cm (1¼ in) above the eyes. Continue making and sewing on loops in this way across the forehead, down the side and round the back of the head until there is a complete looped fringe as shown in diagram 12.

When the doll's head is to be left bare, continue

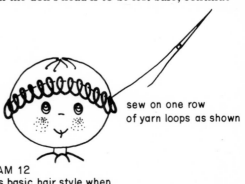

sew on one row
of yarn loops as shown

DIAGRAM 12
the boys basic hair style when
a head covering is to be worn

14

sewing on further rows of looped fringe above the first until the head is completely covered. Now sew down all the loops here and there as shown in diagram 13.

Any variations in these basic styles will be noted in the instructions for individual mascots.

DIAGRAM 13 the boys basic hair style when the head is to be left bare

To make the girl's basic hair style   If the head of the doll is to be covered, only the front portion of the hair is required.

First sew a few loops of yarn to the centre of the forehead 4 cm (1½ in) above the eyes for a fringe. Cut twelve 40 cm (16 in) lengths of yarn and back stitch the centre of the strands to the centre parting position on the head, covering the top of the fringe.

back stitch centre of
yarn strands here

sew the strands
in bunches here

DIAGRAM 14
the girls basic hair style when
a head covering is to be worn

Gather the strands to each side of the head and sew in place, level with the mouth as shown in diagram 14. The hair may now be left in bunches, trimmed shorter, plaited, or as set out in the instructions for the individual doll.

If the doll's head is to be left bare, continue sewing on strands of yarn over the top and down the back of the head as shown in diagram 15. Leave the hair loose or finish as directed in the individual mascot instructions.

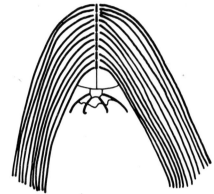

DIAGRAM 15 the girls basic hair style when the head is to be left bare

press the darning needle
against the arm

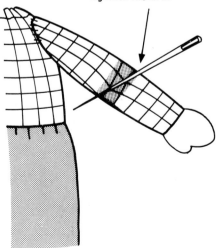

DIAGRAM 16 bending the arm at the elbow

15

To pose the doll's arms   The arms on most of the mascots are bent at the elbows. To do this, press a darning needle against the arm as shown in diagram 16. Fold the arm against the needle, then either sew the palm of the hand to the doll's side to hold it in place or slip stitch the fold in the arm as shown in diagram 17.

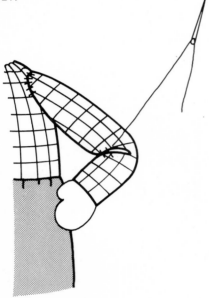

DIAGRAM 17
catch the palm of the hand to
the doll's sides or slip stitch across
the fold in the arm

Cinderella

MATERIALS REQUIRED

Upper body and sleeves — checked or plain fabric and lace edging
Lower body — cream fabric and lace edging
Base — cover with felt to match the lower body
Feet — felt
Skirt — plain or patterned fabric, oddments of brightly coloured fabrics for patches, and tape or ribbon for the waistband
Shawl — plain fabric and a small safety pin
Head scarf — patterned or plain fabric
Broom — a twig or piece of dowelling for handle about 1 cm ($\frac{3}{8}$ in) in diameter by 18cm (7 in) long, plus very thin twigs and strong thread

TO MAKE

Basic doll   Make the basic doll using the fabrics mentioned. Sew on lengths of yarn at the front of the head only and catch them to each side of the head. Cut the strands to even lengths at each side. Make the first mouth stitch as for the basic doll but place the second stitch above the mouth to pull the centre upwards for a sad expression.

Cut the eyes as for the basic doll then cut the eyelids from pink felt as shown on the pattern.

 EYELID

Stick the eyelids to the eyes. Use black thread to make the teardrop on one cheek working a single chain stitch. Work a few tiny stitches in white thread at the lower end of the teardrop for a highlight.

Sew lace edging around the wrists and gather a bit of lace edging around the neck.

Skirt   Cut a 14 cm by 50 cm (5½ in by 20 in) strip of fabric. Cut small patches of fabrics in varying sizes and sew these to the skirt using contrasting coloured thread. Cut the lower edge of the skirt raggedly and rub it to fray out the edges. Join the short edges of the skirt, then gather the remaining raw edge. Put the skirt on the doll, pull up the gathers a little above the waist seam and then fasten off. Sew the gathers to the doll, spacing them out evenly. Place the tape or ribbon round to cover the

The Fairy Godmother

MATERIALS REQUIRED

Upper body and sleeves — satin, lurex or other shiny fabric and lace edging

Lower body — as for the upper body

Base — cover with felt to match the lower body

Feet — felt

Skirt — as for the upper body

Overskirt — net curtain fabric and silver trimming

Cape — as for the overskirt

Hat — as for the upper body

Wand — dowelling about 3 mm ($\frac{1}{8}$ in) in diameter by 14 cm (5½ in) long, silver paper or foil and silver trimming

TO MAKE

Basic doll   Make the basic doll using the fabrics mentioned. Use white yarn for the hair omitting the loops for the fringe and sewing lengths of yarn to the front of the head only. Catch the hair to each side of the head, then wind the strands into coils and sew in place. Stick on the eyes a little higher up the face and closer together than for the basic doll. Sew lace edging round the wrist edges of the sleeves.

Skirt   Cut a 16 cm by 50 cm (6¼ in by 20 in) strip of fabric. Narrowly hem one long edge and sew on lace edging. Join the short edges, then gather the remaining raw edge around the doll's waist. Pull up the gathers and fasten off. Taking care that the hem almost touches the ground, sew the raw edge to the doll, spacing out the gathers evenly.

Overskirt   Cut a 15 cm by 60 cm (6 in by 24 in) strip of fabric. Round off the corners at one long edge, then sew trimming to the short edges, and along this edge. Gather the remaining long edge around the waist, having the short edges meeting at the centre front. Fasten off and then sew the gathers to the doll.

For the waistband cut a 4 cm by 27 cm (1½ in by 10¾ in) strip of fabric. Turn in the long edges to meet each other and press, having the right side of the fabric outside. Place the band in position to cover the gathers, then turn in one end and lap and sew it over the other at the back.

Cape   Cut the cape from fabric. Sew trimming to the front and lower edges, then gather the neck edge around the doll's neck.

gathered raw edge, then turn in one end at the back and lap and sew it over the other end.

Shawl   Cut a 24 cm (9½ in) square of fabric and fray out the raw edges a little. Fold into a triangle and place around the shoulders, pinning the edges together and into the doll at the front as illustrated.

Head scarf   Cut a 25 cm (10 in) square of paper, then fold it in half taking one opposite corner to the other to form a triangle. Use this as a pattern to cut out the scarf, taking care to have the longest edge of the triangle going across the bias of the fabric. Fray out the shorter edges. Turn in the long edge a little and place it it on the head just lapping the hair. Sew the two sharp corners together at the back of the head above the neck, then catch down the remaining corner.

Broom   Place the thin twigs around one end of the handle lapping it about 3 cm (1¼ in). Use strong thread to tie them in place as illustrated.

Place the broom in position against the doll, then bend the arms and fix each hand to the handle as illustrated taking a few stitches around the handle and into each hand.

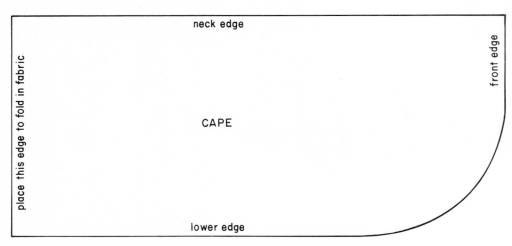

Within the figure: neck edge, front edge, place this edge to fold in fabric, CAPE, lower edge

Hat   Cut a 24 cm by 46 cm (9½ in by 18 in) strip of fabric. Turn in one long edge 6 cm (2½ in) and press, then sew lace edging to the fold. Join the short edges of the hat. Keeping it wrong side out, gather round the remaining long raw edge, taking large running stitches. Pull up the gathers tightly and fasten off, oversewing securely.

Now run a gathering thread round the hat 5 cm (2 in) from the folded edge, then turn it right side out. Put the hat on the doll's head and pull up the gathers to fit as illustrated. Fasten off the thread. Stuff the top of the hat to shape it. Space out the gathers evenly, then catch the hat to the head at the front, back and sides.

Place a narrow strip of net fabric round the hat at the gathers, catching the ends together at the front. Make a bow from net fabric and sew it to the front of the hat, together with a bit of silver trimming.

Wand   Wind a strip of silver paper or foil around the dowelling to cover it, sticking it in place. Gather a bit of silver trimming into a rosette and glue it to one end of the wand. Sew the wand to one of the doll's hands taking the stitches around the wand and into the hand.

Bend the arm as illustrated and sew across the folds.

Miss Priscilla Pringle
the Show Jumper

MATERIALS REQUIRED

Upper body and sleeves — white fabric
Lower body — white fabric
Base — cover with felt to match the feet
Feet — black shiny leather cloth or felt
Hunting tie — white fabric and small gold safety pin
Riding jacket — dark blue felt
Buttons — the buttons on the doll illustrated are
    cut from silver card using a leather punch to make
    perfect circles; alternatively use silver sequins
Hunt cap — dark blue velvet or felt, iron-on inter-
    lining, a 1.5 cm ($\frac{3}{8}$in) diameter trouser button and
    narrow ribbon to match the cap
Riding whip — a wooden cocktail stick, length of
    brown shoe lace, small wooden bead and thin
    cord

TO MAKE

Basic doll   For this doll a smaller base pattern is
given. Make the basic doll using the fabrics mentioned
and easing the lower edge of the body to fit round
the smaller base. Do not make the feet at this stage.

To make the hair cut a 10 cm by 35 cm (4 in by
14 in) strip of very thin card. Wind yarn round the
35 cm (14 in) length of card to cover it. Machine
stitch across, through the centre of the strands, then
tear away the card. Sew the centre machine stitching
to the centre parting position on the doll's head.
Gather all the yarn loops to the back of the head
and tie them together tightly with a narrow ribbon
bow.

For the leg portion of the boots cut a 5 cm by
28 cm (2 in by 11 in) strip of leather cloth or felt.
Join the short ends of the strip and trim the seam.
Put the strip on the doll placing the seam at the
centre back. Sew the lower edge to the base. Now
stitch through the leg portion of the boots at the
centre of the legs in the same way as when dividing
the legs on the basic doll.

Cut four foot pieces from leather cloth using the
show jumper foot pattern. Join the pieces in pairs
round the outer edges taking 3 mm ($\frac{1}{8}$ in) seams.
Trim the seams and turn right side out. Now complete the feet as for the basic doll and sew them in
place having them touching each other at the centre
front.

Hunting tie   Cut a 4 cm by 25 cm (1½ in by 10 in)
strip of fabric. Turn in the long edges to meet each
other and press. Take the strip round the doll's neck
from the front, cross over the ends at the back and
knot once at the front. Fix the tie in place with a
safety pin as illustrated.

Riding jacket   Join all the jacket seams by oversewing the edges of the felt together. Cut the jacket
top from felt. Fold back the lapels at the dotted lines
and press. Join the front shoulder to the back shoulder
edges. Cut one pair of jacket skirt pieces. Join them
to the waist edge of the jacket top matching points
A and B.

Cut two sleeves and join the underarm edges of
each one. Join the armhole edges of the sleeves to the
armholes of the jacket matching points C and D.
Cut two pocket flaps and sew them to the waist seam
of the jacket at the positions indicated on the jacket
skirt pattern.

Cut the jacket back collar piece by the dotted
line shown on the jacket top pattern. Join the
shoulder edges of the front lapels to the shoulder
edges of the back collar. Join the neck edge of the
back collar to the back neck edge of the jacket.

Put the jacket on the doll and lap the right front
slightly over the left front using a little adhesive to
hold it in place. Stick buttons down the jacket front
and one to each sleeve at the lower edge. Stick a
button to each skirt piece as shown on the pattern.

Hunt cap   Iron the interlining onto the wrong side
of the velvet or felt. Cut one pair of cap fronts.
Join the centre front edges taking a 5 mm (¼ in)
seam, then press the seam open. Cut one pair of cap
back pieces and join the centre back edges as for the
fronts. Now join the front to the back at the side
edges taking a 5 mm (¼ in) seam. Press the seam
open. Turn up the lower raw edge of the cap and
slip stitch in place.

Cut two cap peak pieces and join them round
the outer edges taking a 5 mm (¼ in) seam. Trim
the seam, turn and press. Cut a cap peak piece from
thin card. Trim 5 mm (¼ in) off all the edges. Slip
the card piece inside the cap peak and then oversew
the inner edges of the peak together. Slip this edge
just under the front edge of the cap and catch in
place.

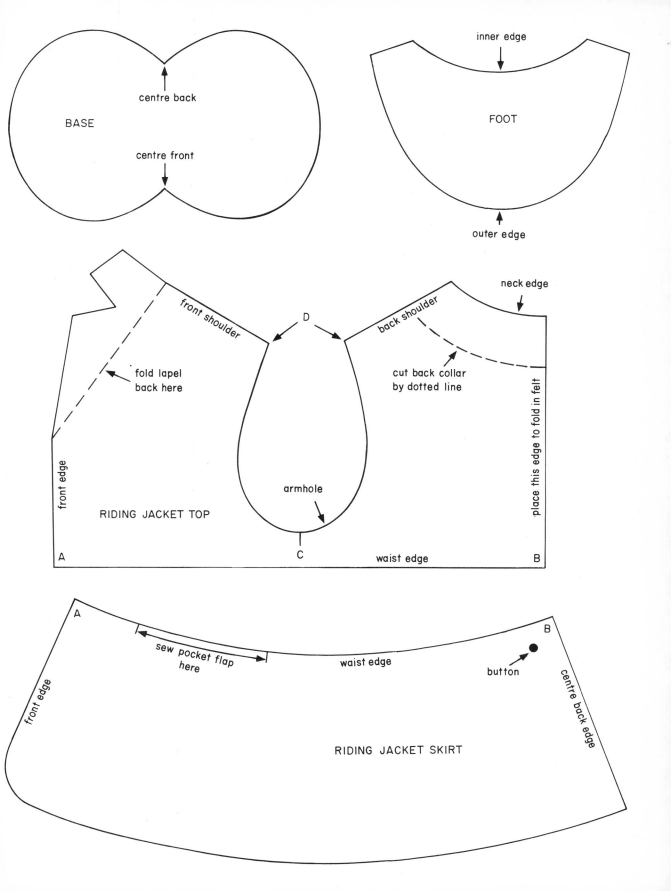

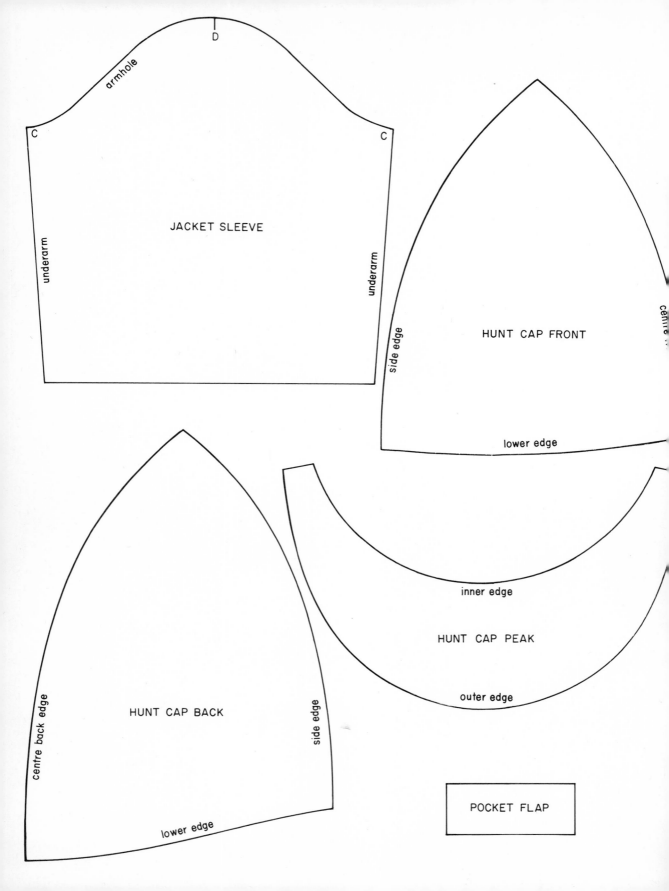

Mr and Mrs Archibald Jones, the bride and groom

Jolly Jack, the pirate, Guardsman Grit of the Coldstream Guards and Olaf the Awful, the Viking

Sylvia Sparkle, the skier

Letitia Love, the tennis
player, Stevie Striker, the
footballer, W.G. Wicket, the
cricketer and Miss Priscilla
Pringle, the show jumper

Stick the rounded face of the button to a piece of velvet or felt and cut out the fabric a little larger all round. Turn and stick this extra material onto the flat face of the button. Now glue the button to the top of the cap. Sew a small ribbon bow to the lower centre back edge of the cap.

Place the cap on the doll's head and catch it in place at the sides and back.

Riding whip   Sandpaper the cocktail stick along the length to taper it towards one end. Push the stick inside the length of shoe lace and trim the lace even with the widest end of the stick. Trim the other end of the lace leaving it 3 cm (1¼ in) longer than the stick. Bend round this extra length to form a loop and wind thread round to hold the cut end of the lace in place, securing the thread end with adhesive.

Make a loop of thin cord for the hand loop and glue the ends to the other end of the stick. Glue this end of the stick into the bead, making the hole in the bead a little larger if necessary.

Sew the whip to the doll's hand taking the stitches around the whip and into the hand. Bend the arms at the elbows and sew the folds in place.

Septimus Neap the Scarecrow

MATERIALS REQUIRED

Upper body and sleeves — striped fabric and odd buttons

Lower body — tweed fabric and oddments of fabric for patches

Base — cover with felt to match the lower body

Feet — felt

Hands — stretchy fabric in any colour, to resemble gloves

Nose — orange felt

Straw — piece of coarsely woven yellow fabric which can be frayed into strands

Waistcoat — fabric or felt

Belt — length of string

Hat — tweed fabric and narrow ribbon

Scarf — checked fabric

TO MAKE

Basic doll Make the basic doll using the fabrics mentioned. When sewing the shoes and hands in place, enclose a few frayed out strands of yellow fabric for bits of straw as illustrated. Instead of yarn for the hair, cut a 10 cm by 26 cm (4 in by 10 in) strip of the yellow fabric. Fray out both long edges leaving about 2 cm (¾ in) unfrayed at the centre of the strip. Snip the frayed out fringe to irregular lengths, then fold the strip in half along the length. Sew the folded edge to the head all round.

Cut out the carrot nose and roll it up as shown on the pattern. Sew the edges to hold them in place and then sew the nose to the face.

Cut the shirt cuffs and fray out all the edges a little. Fold the cuffs in half along the length and sew

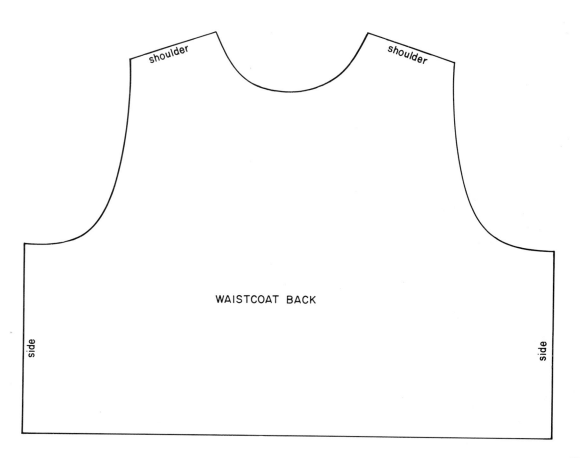

shoulder   shoulder

side   side

WAISTCOAT BACK

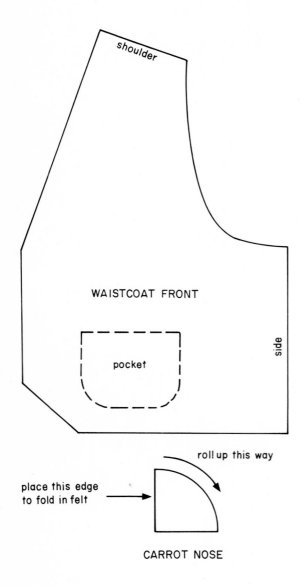

shoulder

WAISTCOAT FRONT

pocket

side

roll up this way

place this edge
to fold in felt →

CARROT NOSE

them around the wrists as illustrated, cutting off any
excess length. Sew the buttons to the shirt. Make a
darn in one of the gloves and sew fabric patches to
one knee and the seat of the pants, enclosing strands
of the yellow fabric.

Snip a slit in the fabric at one elbow, the shirt
front and one leg of the pants and then glue in
bunches of strands of the yellow fabric. Stick a bow
made from string to one shoe.

Belt Tie the string round the doll's waist.

Waistcoat Cut one pair of fronts and one back.
Join them at the side and shoulder edges, then trim
the seams. Stick pockets to the fronts.

Hat Cut out the hat brim and two crown pieces.
Place the brim on the doll's head to cover the top
edge of the hair strip, then sew the inner edge in
place. Join the crown pieces leaving the lower edges
open. Turn right side out and then put it on the
head and sew the lower edge to the inner edge of the
crown, enclosing strands of yellow fabric at intervals.
Indent the crown and catch it to the head. Sew round
the ribbon for the hat band.

Scarf Cut an 8 cm by 38 cm (3 in by 15 in) strip
of fabric and fray out the edges a little. Tie the scarf
round the doll's neck.

Bend the arms at the elbows as illustrated, then
sew the folds in place.

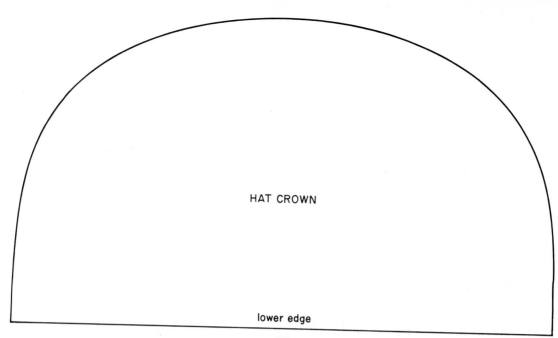

HAT CROWN

lower edge

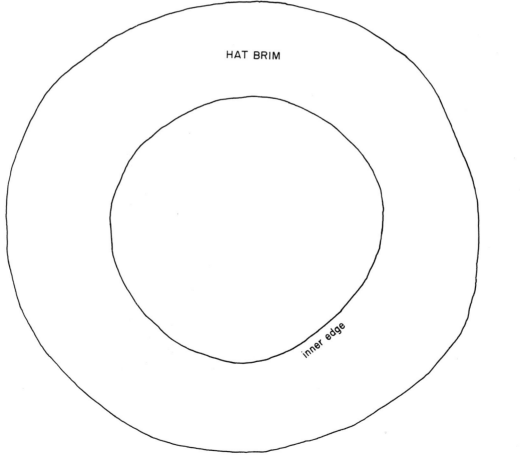

HAT BRIM

inner edge

29

Guardsman Grit
of the Coldstream Guards

MATERIALS REQUIRED

Upper body and sleeves — on the Guardsman this will be the jacket; use red felt for all the pieces including the skirt portion of the jacket

Lower body — black felt and narrow red ribbon for the side seam stripes

Base — cover with felt to match the lower body

Feet — shiny black leather cloth or felt

Collar, cuffs and trimmings — narrow white tape, black and white felt

Buttons — the buttons on the doll illustrated are cut from gold card using a leather punch to make perfect circles; alternatively, use gold sequins

Belt — white felt, narrow gold braid and one small gold button

Bearskin hat — black fur fabric, gold braid for the chin strap and a scrap of red fabric for the plume

TO MAKE

Basic doll   Cut the lower body piece as for the basic doll, then stitch the red ribbon to the piece at the position of each 'side seam' on the finished doll. Fold the ribbon in half along the length if necessary to make the stripe very narrow.

Now make the basic doll using the fabrics mentioned. Omit the hair since the head will be covered by the hat. For the mouth work a small straight stitch only and cut the nose from red felt and then glue in place.

Sleeve cuffs   Cut two cuffs from white felt by the pattern outline and two from black felt as indicated on the cuff pattern. Stick the black pieces to the white pieces as shown. Place a cuff around each wrist as illustrated and oversew the short edges together.

Cuff trimmings   Take care to make a pair of cuff trimmings when sticking all the pieces together. Cut the white felt pieces by the pattern outline and the black felt pieces by the dotted line. For the smaller white felt pieces first cut white felt pieces a little smaller than the black felt pieces, then snip into individual shapes, trimming a little off each to make the gaps between the shapes. Glue all the cuff pieces together, then stick on buttons at the positions of the dots shown on the pattern.

Stick a cuff trimming to each sleeve as illustrated.

Jacket   Cut a 5 cm by 29 cm (2 in by 11½ in) strip of red felt. Run a gathering thread along one long edge and place this around the doll 2 cm (¾ in) above the waist seam. Pull up the gathers to fit, allowing for a small left to right overlap at the front. Sew the gathered edge to the doll.

For the centre front jacket piping use white tape, folding it in half along the length if necessary to make it very narrow. Stick the tape to the doll from the neck edge downwards and along the edge of the jacket skirt.

Back jacket skirt trimmings   These are made in a similar way to the cuff trimmings. Cut black felt pieces by the solid outline of the pattern. Cut the white felt pieces by the dotted lines on the pattern in the same way as for the white felt pieces on the cuffs. Stick all the pieces together and glue on the buttons, then stick the trimmings to the jacket skirt at the back as shown in the illustration. Stick a strip of white tape down the centre back of the jacket skirt in the same way as for the front piping.

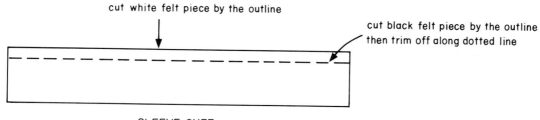

cut white felt piece by the outline

cut black felt piece by the outline
then trim off along dotted line

SLEEVE CUFF

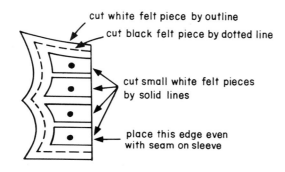

cut white felt piece by outline

cut black felt piece by dotted line

cut small white felt pieces
by solid lines

place this edge even
with seam on sleeve

SLEEVE CUFF TRIMMING

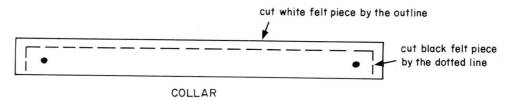

cut white felt piece by the outline

cut black felt piece
by the dotted line

COLLAR

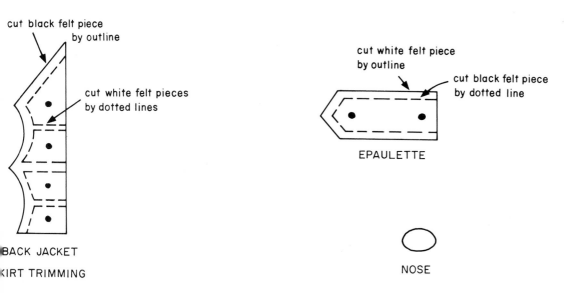

cut black felt piece
by outline

cut white felt pieces
by dotted lines

cut white felt piece
by outline

cut black felt piece
by dotted line

EPAULETTE

BACK JACKET
SKIRT TRIMMING

NOSE

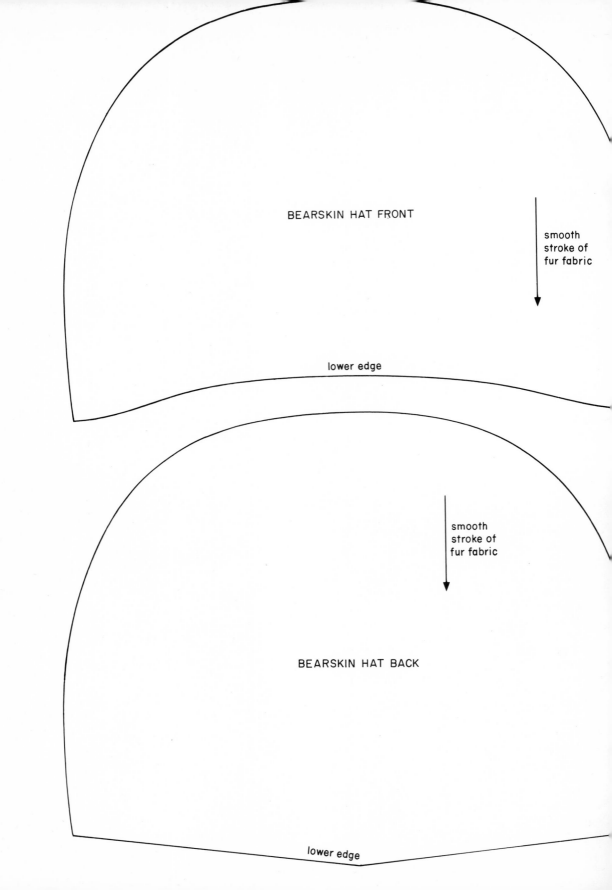

BEARSKIN HAT FRONT

smooth
stroke of
fur fabric

lower edge

smooth
stroke of
fur fabric

BEARSKIN HAT BACK

lower edge

Belt   Cut a 1 cm by 26 cm ($\frac{3}{8}$ in by 10¼ in) strip of white felt. At the centre of the strip sew on the gold button and on either side of this glue a strip of gold braid around the belt as shown in the illustration. Place the belt on the doll to cover the gathered edge of the jacket skirt and sew the short edges of the belt together at the centre back.

Stick another button to the top point of each skirt trimming where it touches the belt as shown in the illustration.

Jacket collar   Cut the collar from white felt by the solid outline on the pattern. Cut another piece from black felt by the dotted line on the pattern, then stick this to the white felt strip. To stiffen the collar glue another piece of white felt to the first piece at the back. Stick on buttons at the positions of the dots on the pattern.

Now place the collar round the doll's neck and stick the shorter ends together at the centre front. The collar should stay in position without sewing to the jacket.

Jacket buttons   Stick eight buttons evenly spaced in pairs down the jacket front, and one single button above the belt buckle as illustrated.

Epaulettes   Make these from white and black felt as for the other pieces as shown on the pattern. Glue on buttons, then stick the epaulettes in place as illustrated.

Bearskin hat   Cut the front and back from fur fabric. Oversew the pieces together round the top edges leaving the lower edges open. Turn in the lower edges a little and slip stitch, pulling the stitches to gather slightly.

Cut a 15 cm (6 in) length of gold braid and stick to the chin and sides of the head as illustrated. Stuff the top of the hat and place it on the doll's head pulling it well down. Catch the lower edge of the hat to the head all round.

For the plume cut a 2.5 cm by 8 cm (1 in by 3 in) strip of red fabric. Fray out one long edge to form a fringe until only a narrow strip of fabric remains. Roll up the strip tightly and stick the end in place. Glue the plume to the right side of the bearskin hat as shown in the illustration.

Do not bend the doll's arms but catch the hands to the trousers at each side as illustrated.

Mr and Mrs Archibald Jones
the Bride and Groom

The Bride

MATERIALS REQUIRED

Upper body and sleeves — white fabric, lace
   trimming, narrow lace edging and ribbon
Lower body — white fabric and lace edging
Base — cover with felt to match the lower body
Feet — white felt
Skirt — white fabric and lace trimming to match
   the upper body
Wedding ring — thick gold thread
Veil — white curtain net and narrow lace edging
Head dress — two small sprays of fabric flowers
Bouquet — a few fabric flowers
Lucky horse shoe — a silver wedding cake decoration
   and white ribbon

TO MAKE

Basic doll   Make the basic doll using the fabrics
mentioned. Sew on strands of yarn at the front of
the head and catch them to the sides, then take them
across the back of the head above the neck and sew
the ends in place, crossing one lot of strands over
the other. Repeat this with another lot of strands to
cover the head completely, tucking in the cut ends
of the yarn. Sew a small twisted ringlet of yarn to
each side of the head tucking it underneath the hair.

Dress   For the dress skirt cut an 18 cm by 40 cm
(7 in by 16 in) strip of fabric. Narrowly hem one
40 cm (16 in) edge. Gather the lace trimming and sew
it to the skirt, having the lower edge of the lace and
hem even. Join the short edges of the skirt. Gather
the remaining raw edge, put the skirt on the doll and
pull up the gathers. Make sure that the skirt hem
touches the ground; then sew the gathered raw edge
to the doll, spacing out the gathers evenly all round.
Sew narrow lace edging round the gathered raw edge
of the skirt for the waistband, and round the wrist
edges of the sleeves.

   For the neck frill gather a 38 cm (15 in) length
of lace trimming round the neck and fasten off. Lap
and sew the short edges of the trimming at the back
of the doll. Sew a ribbon bow to the frill below the
chin.

Veil   Cut a 50 cm by 85 cm (20 in by 34 in) piece
of net fabric. Round off all the corners making large
curves. Sew narrow lace edging all round the edges
of the veil. Turn back one 50 cm (20 in) edge as
shown in the diagram and gather along the fold,

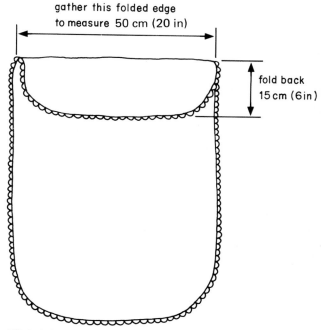

gather this folded edge
to measure 50 cm (20 in)

fold back
15 cm (6 in)

FOLDING THE VEIL

pulling up the gathers to measure 15 cm (6 in).
Fasten off the thread. Sew this gathered edge to the
top of the doll's head as illustrated.

Head dress   Twist the sprays of fabric flowers
together, then sew to the head at the gathered edge
of the veil as illustrated.

Bouquet   Twist the stems of the fabric flowers
together forming a bunch. Bend the stems to fit
around the doll's hand and then sew in place.

Lucky horse shoe   Stick a loop of ribbon to the top
of the horse shoe to fit over the doll's hand.

Wedding ring   Thread a needle with the gold thread. Take a stitch through the left hand at the position of the third finger, then knot the thread ends at the other side of the hand. Secure the knot with a dab of adhesive. Bend the arms as illustrated and sew across the folds.

The Groom

MATERIALS REQUIRED
Upper body and sleeves — white fabric
Lower body — black and white, or black and grey striped fabric or plain grey
Base — cover with felt to match the lower body
Feet — black felt
Shirt collar — white fabric
Necktie — 10 cm (4 in) length of narrow grey ribbon
Waistcoat — grey felt and four small buttons
Tailcoat — black or grey felt
Buttonhole — small fabric or dried flower
Top hat — grey felt, thin card, iron-on interlining and narrow black ribbon

TO MAKE
Basic doll   Make the basic doll using the fabrics mentioned. Make cuffs on the shirt sleeves. For the hair sew on a single looped fringe.

Necktie   Tie the ribbon in a loose knot at the centre of the length and sew the knot to the shirt below the chin as illustrated.

Shirt collar   Cut a 6 cm by 10 cm (2 $\frac{3}{8}$ in by 4 in) strip of white fabric. Turn in all the raw edges and press, then fold the collar bringing the long edges together and slip stitch the edges all round. Place the collar around the neck and catch the two lower corners together beneath the necktie.

Waistcoat   Cut out the waistcoat front. Sew the buttons down the centre front then place the waistcoat on the doll and sew the shoulders and side edges in place.

Tailcoat   Join all the tailcoat seams by oversewing the edges together. Cut out the tailcoat, then cut open the back at the fold as shown on the pattern. Sew the front shoulder edges to the back shoulder edges. Cut two sleeves and join the underarm edges of each one. Place the armholes of the sleeves to the armholes of the coat and sew in place matching points A and B. Turn the coat right side out, fold back the lapels and press. Cut the back collar as

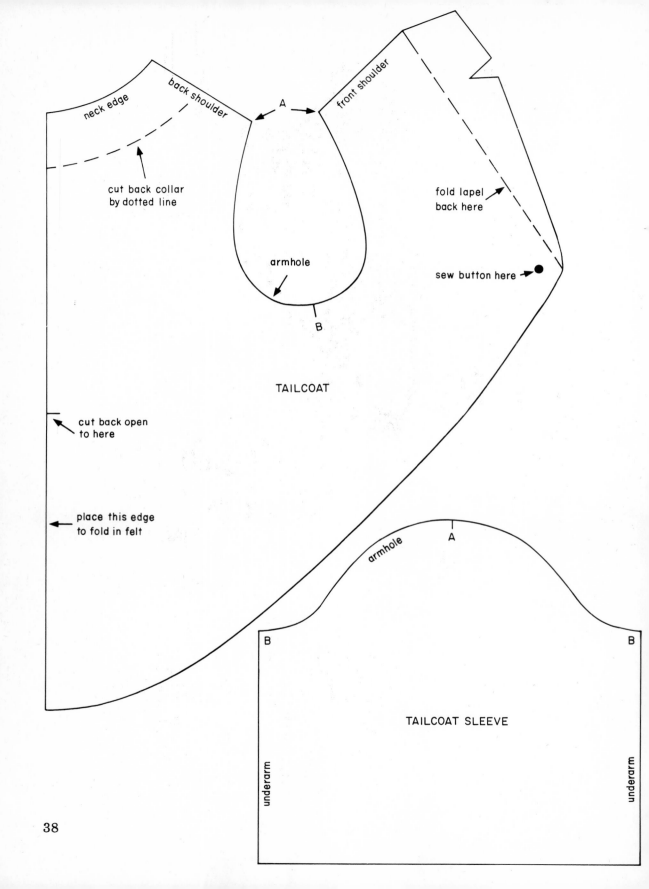

neck edge

back shoulder

A

front shoulder

cut back collar
by dotted line

fold lapel
back here

armhole

sew button here ●

B

TAILCOAT

cut back open
to here

place this edge
to fold in felt

armhole

A

B

B

TAILCOAT SLEEVE

underarm

underarm

38

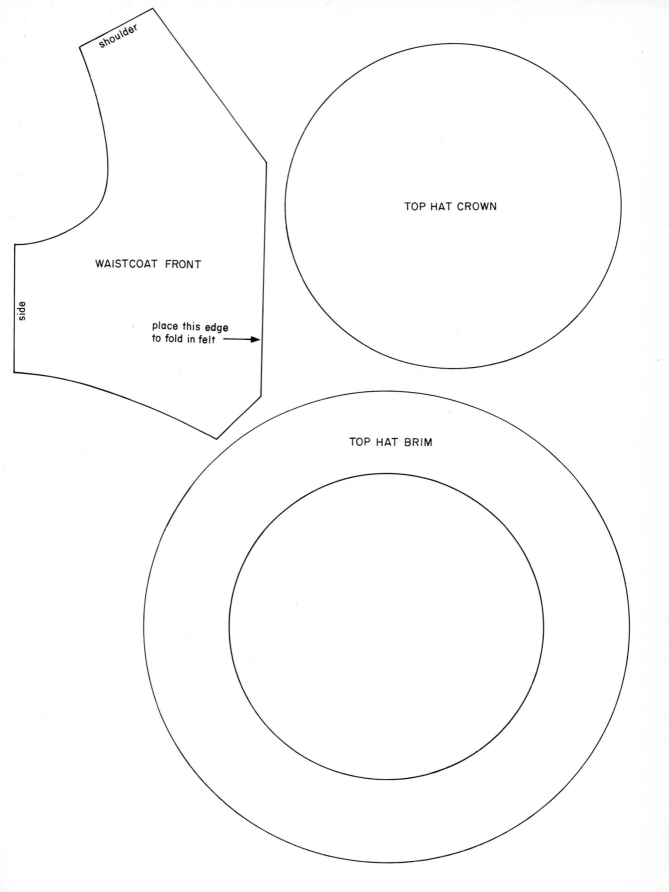

shoulder

WAISTCOAT FRONT

side

place this edge
to fold in felt →

TOP HAT CROWN

TOP HAT BRIM

shown by the dotted line on the coat pattern, join the shoulder edges of the collar to the front lapels, then sew the neck edge of the back collar to the neck edge of the coat. Put the coat on the doll and stick the buttonhole to the left lapel.

Top hat Cut two hat brim pieces from felt. Cut one hat brim piece from thin card, then trim 3 mm ($\frac{1}{8}$ in) off the outer and inner edges. Stick the card brim between the felt brim pieces, then stitch all round the brim close to the outer edge. Cut a 5 cm by 26 cm (2 in by 10¼ in) strip of felt for the hat side piece. Stretch one long edge of the strip slightly to obtain the flared-out shape of the top of the hat. Iron interlining onto the felt strip, then cut out the interlining even with the felt. Join the short edges, taking a tiny seam.

Cut the hat crown piece and iron on interlining as for the hat side. Place the crown on top of the hat side piece having the wrong side outside. Oversew the edges together. Turn the hat right side out. Cut a circle of card a little smaller than the crown, spread on a little adhesive and push it inside the hat against the crown. Oversew the lower edge of the hat to the inner edge of the brim. Stick the ribbon hat band round the hat as illustrated. Curl up the brim at each side by rolling it round a pencil. Glue the hat to the doll's head, lapping it over the top edge of the hair loops.

Bend the arms and catch the hands to the doll at each side as illustrated.

40

Stevie Striker
the Footballer

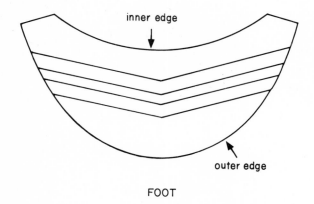

inner edge

outer edge

FOOT

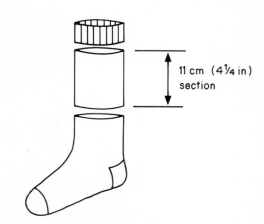

11 cm (4¼ in) section

DIAGRAM showing how to cut the football sock piece

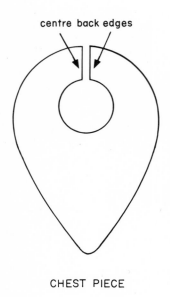

centre back edges

CHEST PIECE

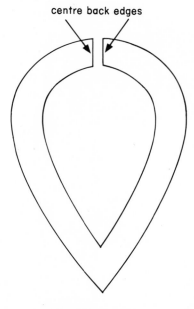

centre back edges

SHIRT COLLAR

42

MATERIALS REQUIRED

Upper body and sleeves — fabric and felt in the desired club colours, adding any extra stripes or cuff pieces after making the basic doll

Lower body — flesh-coloured felt

Base — cover with felt to match the feet

Feet — black and white felt and narrow tape

Chest piece — flesh-coloured felt

Socks — Cutting from a man's sock in the desired club colour

Shorts — fabric in the desired club colour and narrow elastic, adding any extra stripes before sewing the shorts in place on the doll

TO MAKE

Basic doll Make the basic doll using the fabrics mentioned, but not the feet. For the hair sew on loops of yarn to cover the head completely.

For the football socks cut an 11 cm (4¼ in) section off the leg of the sock as shown in the diagram. Place this around the doll's legs having the lower edge just above the base. Slip stitch this edge to the doll. Turn down the upper edge of the sock piece 2 cm (¾ in) twice. Now stitch through the sock piece at the centre of the legs in the same way as when dividing the legs on the basic doll.

To make each knee, take a tiny secure stitch 1 cm ($\frac{3}{8}$ in) above the top edge of the sock and 1 cm ($\frac{3}{8}$ in) away from the centre stitching line. Pass the needle across and through the leg bringing it out 3 cm (1¼ in) away from the first stitch. Pass the needle back again and pull the thread up tight to form the knee. Fasten off the thread.

For the sides of the football boots cut a 2 cm by 27 cm (¾ in by 10½ in) strip of black felt. Oversew the short edges together, then place the strip around the legs with the seam at the back and oversew one long edge to the edge of the base. Sew through the centre of the strip as for the socks.

Make the feet as for the basic doll using the footballer foot pattern. Sew them in place having them touching each other at the centre front. Stick on narrow strips of felt for the stripes as shown on the pattern and bows of tape for the laces.

Chest piece Cut the chest piece from felt and sew it to the doll joining the centre back edges at the back.

Shirt collar Cut the collar from felt and stick it in place joining the centre back edges at the back.

Shorts Cut an 8 cm by 32 cm (3¼ in by 12½ in) strip of fabric. Turn in one long raw edge 5 mm (¼ in) and stitch down. Make a narrow hem on the remaining long raw edge and thread through elastic to fit round the doll's waist. Join the short edges of the strip, noting that this seam will be at the centre back of the doll.

Place the shorts on the doll with the elastic round the waist. Catch the lower edge of the shorts at the centre front to the centre back seam, taking the stitches through the doll in the same way as when dividing the legs on the basic doll.

Bend the arms and sew across the folds to hold in position.

Laura May and Cousin Zeke
Country Cousins

Laura May

MATERIALS REQUIRED

Upper body and sleeves — large checked gingham
   fabric, lace edging and three small buttons
Lower body — white fabric and lace edging
Base — cover with felt to match the lower body
Feet — stockinette to match the head and hands
Skirt — fabric as for the upper body
Skirt frill, shoulder frills and waistband — small
   checked gingham fabric

TO MAKE

Basic doll   Make the basic doll except for the feet,
using the fabrics mentioned. Sew on strands of yarn
to completely cover the head, then stroke the
strands down smoothly all round the head. Trim the
ends to an even length. Stick the strands to the head
lifting them a few at a time and spreading the head
with adhesive.

Decorate the hair with a few guipure flowers or
a ribbon bow. Use the moistened point of a brown
pencil to mark on the freckles above the nose.

Cut two pairs of foot pieces from stockinette
using the bare foot pattern. Join the pieces in pairs
taking 3 mm ($\frac{1}{8}$ in) seams and leaving the inner edges
open. Trim the seams and turn the feet right side
out. Turn in the inner edges 5 mm ($\frac{1}{4}$ in) and tack
loosely. Stuff the feet lightly and sew them in place
as for the basic doll's feet. Make the toes by working
four stitches around and through each foot as shown
in the illustration, using matching thread.

Dress   For the shoulder frills cut two 5 cm by 30 cm
(2 in by 12 in) strips of fabric. Narrowly hem one
long edge of each strip, then turn in the other long
raw edge and gather to fit over each shoulder from
the centre front waist to the centre back waist. Sew
the frill ends in place.

For the skirt cut an 8 cm by 60 cm (3 in by 24 in)
strip of fabric. For the hem frill cut a 6 cm by 90 cm
(2½ in by 36 in) strip of fabric. Make the frill as for
the shoulder frills, gathering it to fit the skirt. Lap
the gathered edge of the frill 1 cm ($\frac{3}{8}$ in) over one
long edge of the skirt and sew in place. Join the
short edges of the skirt and frill. Gather the remaining
raw edge and place the skirt on the doll, pulling up

the gathers tightly a little above the waist seam.
Fasten off the thread and then space out the gathers
evenly and sew the raw edge to the body.

For the waistband cut a 4 cm by 27 cm (1½ in by
10¾ in) strip of fabric. Turn in the long edges to meet
each other and press. Place the waistband in position
to cover the raw edges of the skirt, then turn in one
end and lap and sew it over the other end at the back.

Sew lace edging around each wrist and gather a
strip of lace edging around the neck. Sew the buttons
down the front of the bodice.

Bend the arms and sew across the folds to hold
in place, then sew the hands to the skirt as illustrated.

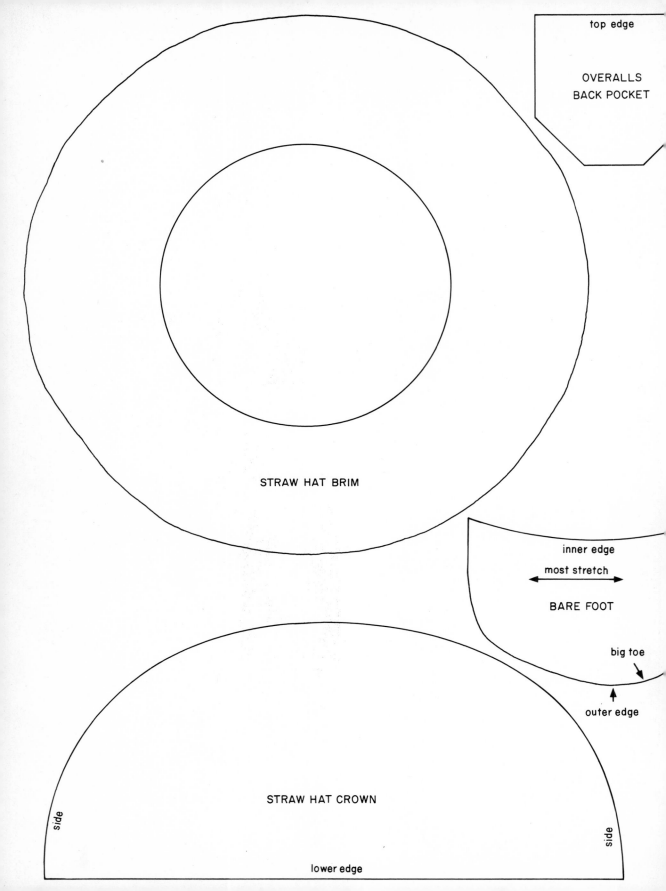

top edge

OVERALLS
BACK POCKET

STRAW HAT BRIM

inner edge

most stretch

BARE FOOT

big toe

outer edge

STRAW HAT CROWN

side

side

lower edge

Cousin Zeke

MATERIALS REQUIRED

Upper body and sleeves — checked fabric
Lower body — denim fabric or cuttings off old
   jeans, plus oddments of fabric for the knee
   patches
Base — cover with felt to match the lower body
Feet — stockinette to match the head and hands
Overall bib and straps —fabric to match the lower
   body plus two small buttons
Scarf — plain or patterned fabric
Straw hat — fabric with a straw-like texture and
   colour

TO MAKE

Basic doll   Make the basic doll except for the
feet, using the fabrics mentioned. Make cuffs on the
shirt sleeves. For the hair sew on a single looped
fringe and place the mouth stitch a little off centre
as illustrated. Mark on freckles and make the feet in
the same way as for Laura May.

Overalls   For the bib cut a 6 cm by 8 cm (2½ in by
3¼ in) piece of fabric. Turn in all the raw edges
except for one 8 cm (3¼ in) edge and slip stitch
them in place. Sew the remaining raw edge to the top
edge of the pants at the centre front.

For the shoulder straps cut two 3 cm by 17 cm
(1¼ in by 6¾ in) strips of fabric. Turn in the long
edges to meet each other on each strip and press,
having the right side of the fabric outside. Slip one
end of each strap under the top corners of the bib,
and sew in place at the same time as sewing the
buttons in position as illustrated.

Take the straps to the back waist edge crossing
them over each other at the back. Sew to the waist
seam, trimming off any excess length. Make the
waistband as for the shoulder straps using a 3 cm by
27 cm (1¼ in by 10¾ in) strip of fabric. Put the
waistband in position, then turn in one short edge
and lap and sew it over the other at the back.

Cut two 4 cm (1½ in) squares of fabric for the
knee patches. Fray out all the raw edges a little and
sew the patches in place on the doll as illustrated.
Cut two back pockets, turn in the top edges 5 mm
(¼ in) and sew down. Turn in the remaining raw
edges 5 mm (¼ in) and tack, then sew the pockets
to the seat of the overalls just below the waistband.

Straw hat   Glue two layers of the hat fabric
together, then cut out the hat brim. Spread the inner
edge with adhesive to seal the raw edges and then
rub the outer edges to fray them out slightly.

Cut two hat crown pieces from fabric and join
them, leaving the lower edges open. Trim the seam
and turn the crown right side out. Seal the lower
edges with adhesive as for the hat brim. Now oversew
the lower edge of the crown to the inner edge of the
brim all round. Place the hat on the doll's head
lapping it over the top of the hair. Catch it to the
head all round where the brim joins the crown.
Push in the crown of the hat at each side and catch
it in place taking a stitch through the head.

Scarf   Cut a 20 cm (8 in) square of fabric and then
cut it in half from one corner to the opposite corner,
forming two triangles. Use one piece only. Fray out
the edges a little and tie the scarf round the doll's
neck as illustrated.

Bend the arms at the elbows and sew the folds
in place. Sew one hand to the overall bib and the
other to the waistband.

The Red Avenger, space hero

Septimus Neap, the scarecrow

Mr Topeloff, the clown

Hemlock Soames
the Detective

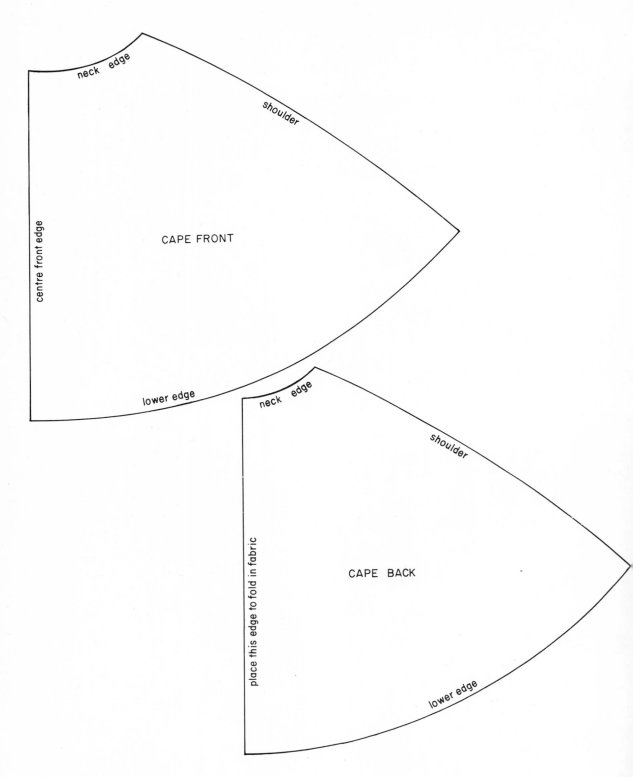

neck edge

shoulder

centre front edge

CAPE FRONT

lower edge

neck edge

shoulder

place this edge to fold in fabric

CAPE BACK

lower edge

50

MATERIALS REQUIRED

Upper body and sleeves — checked or tweedy fabric
Lower body — tweed or plain fabric
Base — cover with felt to match the lower body
Feet — felt
Coat body, cape and collar — as for the upper body,
  plus three small buttons
Cap — checked fabric and ribbon
Magnifying glass — a plastic toy magnifying glass

TO MAKE

Basic doll   Make the basic doll using the fabrics
mentioned but do not sew the arms to the body at
this stage. For the hair sew on a single looped fringe.

Coat body   Cut a 20 cm by 35 cm (8 in by 14 in)
strip of fabric. Turn in the raw edges except for one
long edge and slip stitch them in place. Gather the
long raw edge and pull up the gathers to fit around
the doll's neck, lapping the left front edge about
2 cm (¾ in) over the right front edge at the front.
Fasten off the thread and sew the lapped portions
together at the neck edges. Sew the buttons down the
front through both thicknesses of fabric spacing them
as illustrated. Now sew the arms in position taking
the stitches through the coat fabric and into the
body. Catch the arms close to the body at the under-
arms.

Cape   Cut one cape back piece and one pair of front
pieces. Join the fronts to the back at the shoulder
edges, then press the seams open. Turn in the lower
and centre front raw edges and slip stitch in place.
Put the neck edge of the cape around the doll's
neck and sew the centre front neck edges together.

Collar   Cut out the collar, turn in the raw edges
3 mm ($\frac{1}{8}$ in) and slip stitch, clipping the neck edge
curve if necessary. Place the collar round the doll's
neck and catch points A together at the centre front.

Cap   Cut four cap section pieces and join them in
pairs at one side edge. Press the seams open. Now
join the pairs together at the remaining side edges
and press the seams open. Turn in the lower edge of
the cap and slip stitch in place.

  For each ear flap cut two cap section pieces. Join
them round the edges leaving a gap for turning. Trim
the seams, turn right side out and slip stitch the gap,
then press. Catch the lower edge of each ear flap to
the lower edge of the cap at each side. Sew the top
points of the flaps to the top of the cap, then sew
on a ribbon bow.

  For each cap peak, one for the front and one for
the back, cut two peak pieces. Join them round the
outer edges and then trim the seams. Turn right side

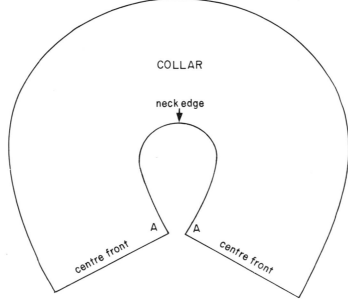

COLLAR

neck edge

A   A

centre front   centre front

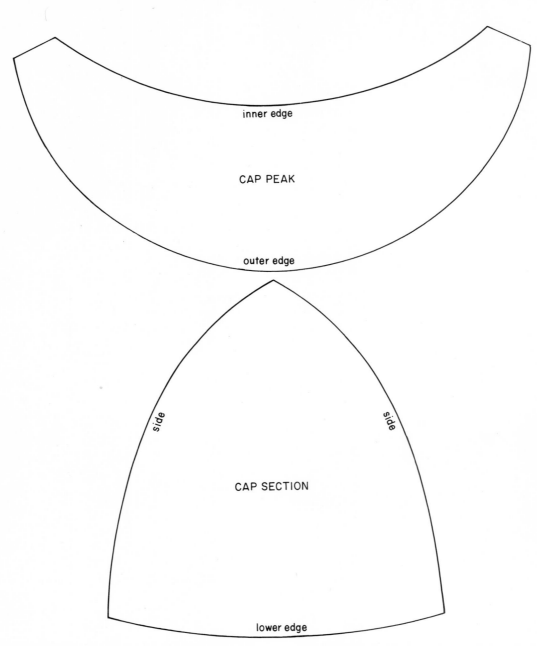

inner edge

CAP PEAK

outer edge

side

side

CAP SECTION

lower edge

out and press. Oversew the inner raw edges of each cap peak together. Slip the raw edges of each cap peak 5 mm (¼ in) under the lower edge of the cap, having the ends of the peaks meeting at each side of the cap. Slip stitch the lower edge of the cap to the peaks.

Stuff the top of the cap and then place it on the doll's head, lapping it over the top of the hair. Sew the cap to the head at each side.

Magnifying glass   Sew the handle to one hand taking the stitches round the handle and into the hand. Bend the arms at the elbows and sew the folds in place.

Miss Felicity Fanshaw the Edwardian Lady

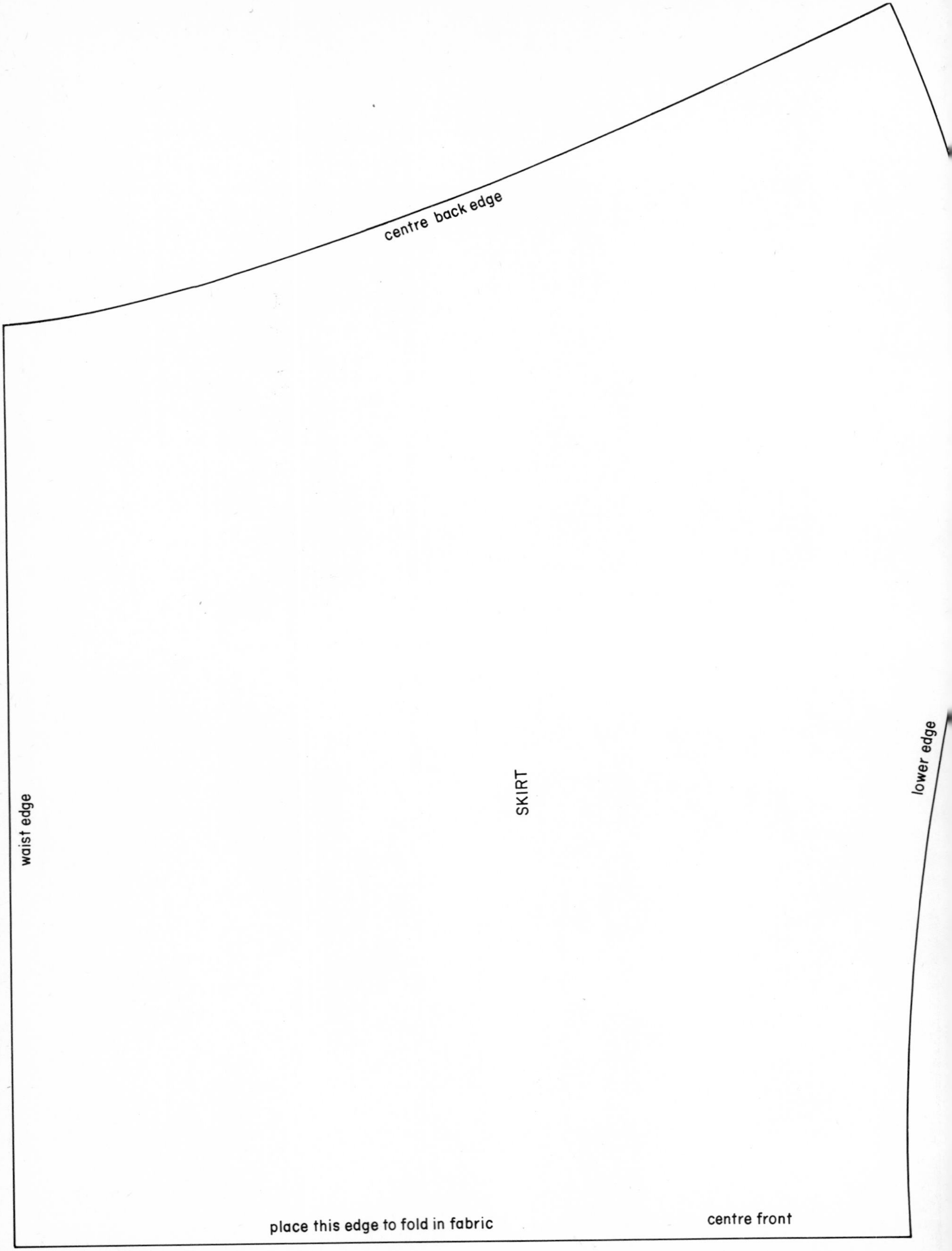

centre back edge

SKIRT

waist edge

lower edge

place this edge to fold in fabric

centre front

MATERIALS REQUIRED

Upper body and sleeves — plain silky fabric and
narrow lace edging

Lower body — to match the upper body

Base — cover with felt to match the lower body

Feet — omit the feet since they will spoil the line of
the dress on the finished doll

Dress skirt — to match the upper body

Dress trimming and belt — pleated or ruffled
trimming about 5 cm (2 in) in width, lace edging
about 4 cm (1¾ in) in width and narrow ribbon

Hat — felt, strong paper and trimmings as available,
such as feathers, fabric flowers, leaves and ribbon
bows

Walking stick — a 14 cm (5½ in) length of 5 mm
(¼ in) diameter wooden dowelling, black marker
pen and narrow gold braid

TO MAKE

Basic doll   Make the basic doll using the fabrics
mentioned and omitting the feet. When sewing the
neck in place leave a little more of the neck piece
exposed to leave room for the high collar. Sew
narrow lace edging round each wrist edge of the
sleeve.

For the hair use mohair or similar yarn instead of
chunky or double knitting. To make the upswept
hair style, cut a 10 cm by 24 cm (4 in by 10½ in)
strip of strong paper. Wind the yarn loosely round
the width of the paper to cover it completely. Now
machine stitch all along one edge of the paper
catching the yarn loops as close to the edge as
possible. At the other long edge, thread a long length
of yarn through all the loops leaving enough length
at each end so that the loops will not slip off. Tear
away the paper strip.

Pin the machined edge across the doll's forehead,
down the sides of the face and across the back of the
head, having the yarn loops hanging downwards.
Back stitch the machined edge to the head as pinned.

Now take the ends of the length of yarn and pull
up and knot very tightly, thus bringing the loops
to the top of the doll's head. Sew the knotted yarn
to the head.

Dress skirt   Cut out the skirt and make a narrow
hem on the lower edge. Sew pleated or frilled trimming to the skirt having the lower edges even and easing
the trimming round the curves. Sew lace trimming
to the skirt having one long edge just lapping the
other trimming.

Now join the centre back edges of the skirt. Run
a gathering thread round the waist edge, put the skirt
on the doll, pull up the gathers round the waist and
fasten off. Pull all the gathers to the back and sides
of the skirt leaving the front quite smooth. Sew the
waist edge to the doll.

Collar   Cut the collar from thick white paper and
cover it by glueing round a piece of lace edging.
Place the collar round the doll's neck and sew the
centre back edges together.

Dress trimming   Cut a 40 cm (16 in) length each of
pleated and lace trimming. Lay the lace on top of
the trimming having them even at one long edge, and
then sew them together at this edge. Now gather a
10 cm (4 in) portion at the centre of this edge, pull
up the gathers tightly and fasten off. Sew this
gathered portion to the doll at the centre front about
4 cm (1½ in) down from the collar, then sew on a
ribbon bow. Pin the lengths of trimming over each
shoulder to the back waist edge, then trim off any
excess. Sew the trimming to the bodice and back
waist edge.

Belt   Cut a piece of trimming or lace to go round
the doll's waist. Fold to make a 1.5 cm (½ in) width,
then place round the waist and sew the edges together
at the front underneath the dress trimming.

COLLAR

centre back

centre back

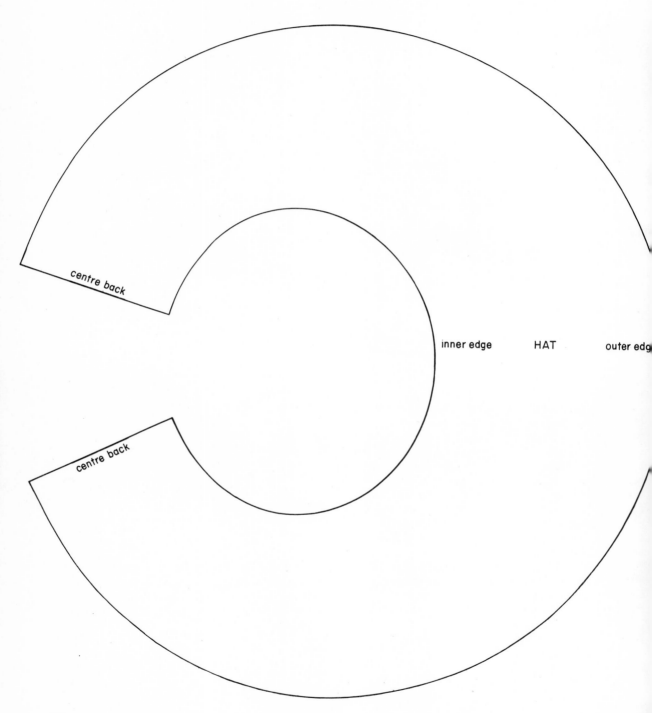

centre back

centre back

inner edge   HAT   outer edg

56

Hat Cut two hat pieces from felt and one from strong paper. Trim 5 mm (¼ in) off the edges of the paper all round. Stick the paper piece between the felt pieces. Now stitch round close to the outer and inner edges of the felt. Join the centre back edges by oversewing them together. Sew guipure flowers round the outer edge of the hat.

Place the hat on the doll's head and catch the inner edge to the head to hold in place. Sew the available trimmings to the top of the head to cover it completely, thus forming the crown of the hat.

Walking stick Colour the dowelling with marker pen. Stick the braid round the top 2 cm (¾ in) of the stick to cover it, then glue braid round and round the top to form the 'knob'. When the adhesive is dry, sew the knob to the doll's hand taking the stitches through the braid and into the hand. Bend the other arm and sew the fold in place.

Mr Topeloff the Clown

MATERIALS REQUIRED

Upper body and sleeves — plain and striped fabric
  and three small pom-poms or buttons
Lower body — checked fabric
Base — cover with felt to match the lower body
Feet — leather or leather cloth, felt, thin card, marker
  pen and ribbon
Wig — long pile fur fabric
Hat — black felt, thin card, braid, a guipure flower
  and green felt
Bow tie — fancy ribbon
Braces — felt and four buttons
Umbrella — plastic knitting needle, felt and scraps
  of fabric

TO MAKE

Basic doll   Make the basic doll using the fabrics
mentioned except for the feet. Sew the pom-poms
or buttons to the shirt front as illustrated and make
striped cuffs on the sleeves.

Cut two foot upper pieces from leather or leather
cloth. On the right side mark on all the details shown
on the pattern with marker pen. On the wrong side
oversew the curved edges together at the toe as shown
on the pattern. Turn the uppers right side out. Cut
two foot soles from two layers of felt glued together.
Place an upper against each sole, right sides outside,
then stitch them together close to the edges leaving
the inner edges open.

Cut two innersoles from thin card as shown by the
dotted line on the sole pattern. Slip one inside each
foot against the soles, bending the card slightly in
order to get it through the inner edges. Now stuff
the feet and sew them in place as for the basic doll.
Sew a ribbon bow to each foot as illustrated.

Wig   For the wig cut a 4 cm by 20 cm (1½ in by 8 in)
strip of long pile fur fabric. Turn in the short edges
1 cm ($\frac{3}{8}$ in) and sew down. Pin the strip to the doll's
head about 4 cm (1½ in) down from the gathered
top. Sew the top edge of the strip to the head.

Cut all the facial features from felt in the colours
indicated on the patterns. Work the mouth stitches
on the felt mouth piece in the same way as for the
basic doll. Stick all the face pieces in position as
illustrated, colouring the cheeks with pencil before
glueing on the mouth piece.

Hat   Cut two brim pieces from felt, cut one brim
piece from thin card, then trim 5 mm (¼ in) off the
outer and inner edges. Stick the card piece between
the felt pieces. Stitch all round close to the outer
and inner edges of the felt brim.

For the hat side piece cut a 5 cm by 22 cm (2 in
by 8¾ in) strip of felt. Oversew the short edges
together, then oversew one long edge to the inner
edge of the hat brim.

Cut the hat crown from thin card and stick it to
a piece of felt. Cut out the felt 5 mm (¼ in) larger
all round than the card. Snip the felt round the edges
and turn onto the other side of the card, then stick
down. Place the crown on top of the hat and catch
in place all round.

For the flower stalk cut a 1 cm by 6 cm ($\frac{3}{8}$ in by
2½ in) strip of green felt. Oversew the long edges
together, then sew one end to the back of the guipure
flower. Cut the leaf from green felt and sew it to the
stalk. Sew the stalk to the hat. Glue the braid round
the hat for the hat band.

Stick the hat to the doll's head to cover the top
edge of the wig.

Bow tie   Tie the ribbon round the doll's neck
making a large bow at the front.

Braces   Cut two braces from felt and pin to the
pants top at the front and back taking one over each
shoulder and crossing them over at the back. Sew the
buttons in place on the braces as illustrated, taking
the stitches through the braces and into the doll.

Umbrella   Cut the top off the knitting needle
making it about 16 cm (6¼ in) in length. Heat the top
end of the length in very hot water and then gently
bend to the curved handle shape. Cut the umbrella
from felt using the pattern. Stick on a few small
patches of fabric. Oversew the edges together as
indicated on the pattern. Slip the umbrella onto the
handle and glue the lower end to the handle as
illustrated. Gather round the top of the umbrella as
shown on the pattern, pull up the gathers and fasten
off.

Sew the handle to the doll's hand taking the
stitches round the handle and into the hand. Bend the
arm as shown and sew across the fold.

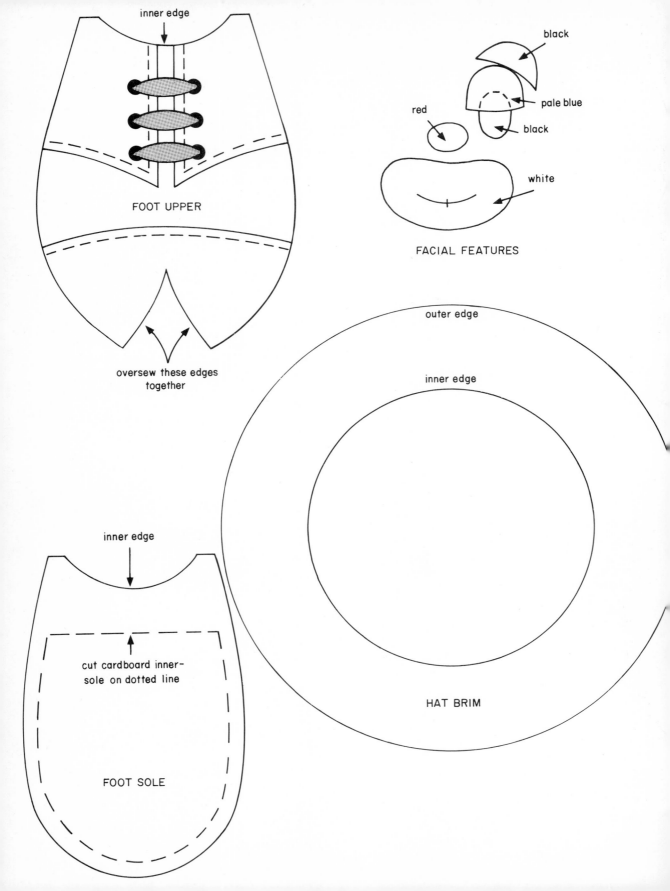

inner edge

FOOT UPPER

oversew these edges
together

black

pale blue

red

black

white

FACIAL FEATURES

outer edge

inner edge

inner edge

cut cardboard inner-
sole on dotted line

FOOT SOLE

HAT BRIM

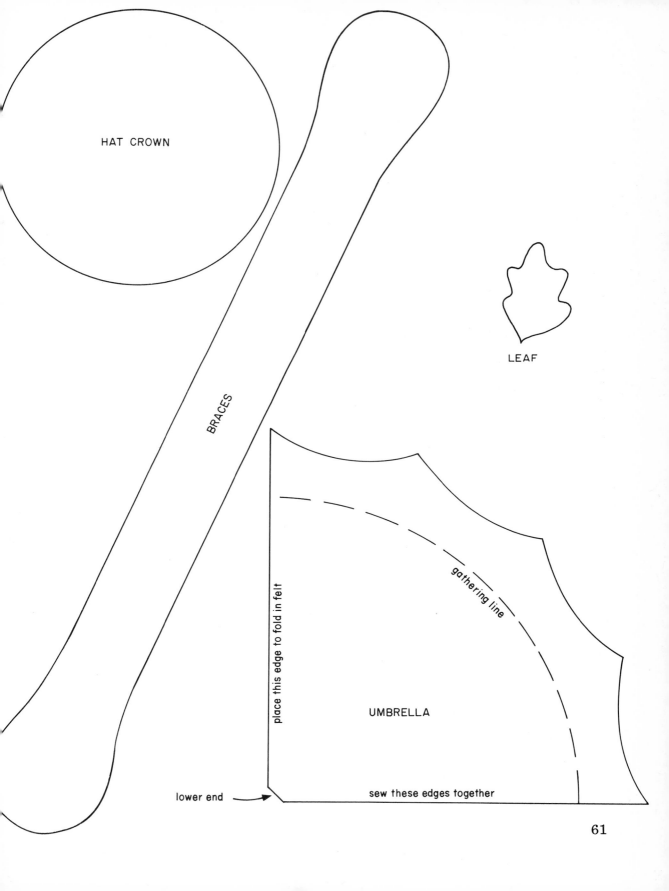

HAT CROWN

LEAF

BRACES

place this edge to fold in felt

gathering line

UMBRELLA

lower end →

sew these edges together

61

Wild Bill Hickory the Frontiersman

MATERIALS REQUIRED

Upper body and sleeves — on the frontiersman this will be the buckskin shirt; use chamois leather or similar coloured felt for all the pieces including the pockets, fringes and skirt portion of the shirt

Lower body — to match the upper body

Base — cover to match the lower body

Feet — brown felt

Belt — brown leather cloth or felt and a small buckle

Neckerchief — red fabric

'Coon skin cap — light brown fur or fur fabric and black marker pen

TO MAKE

Basic doll   Make the basic doll using the fabrics mentioned except for the feet. Omit the hair since the cap will cover the head. Place the mouth stitch a little off centre as illustrated.

Make the feet as for the basic doll using the frontiersman foot pattern, and sew them in place having them touching each other at the centre front. Use dark brown thread to work cross stitches up the front of the shirt as shown in the illustration, then tie the thread at the neck.

Shirt skirt   Cut a 5 cm by 27 cm (2 in by 10¾ in) strip. Make 2 cm (¾ in) deep snips along one long edge at close regular intervals to form the fringe. Sew the unfringed edge round the doll's waist seam joining the short edges at the back.

Pockets   Cut two pockets and sew them to the front of the shirt as illustrated.

Sleeve fringes   Cut two sleeve fringe pieces, then snip them along the edge as indicated on the pattern. Sew the unfringed edges to the arms from the shoulders to the wrists as illustrated.

Belt   Cut a strip the width of the centre bar of the buckle by 30 cm (12 in) in length. Sew one end round the centre bar of the buckle and cut the other end to a V-shape. Place the belt around the doll and fasten at the front.

Neckerchief   Cut two pieces and join them round the edges taking a 5 mm (¼ in) seam and leaving a gap for turning. Trim the corners, turn right side out and slip stitch the gap. Tie round the doll's neck as illustrated.

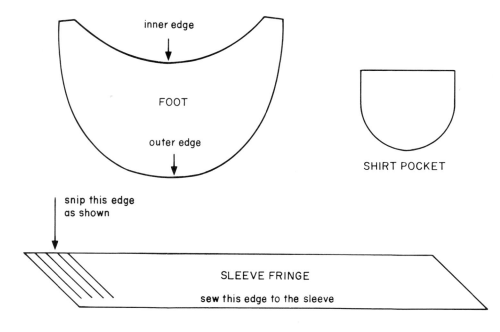

inner edge

FOOT

outer edge

SHIRT POCKET

snip this edge as shown

SLEEVE FRINGE

sew this edge to the sleeve

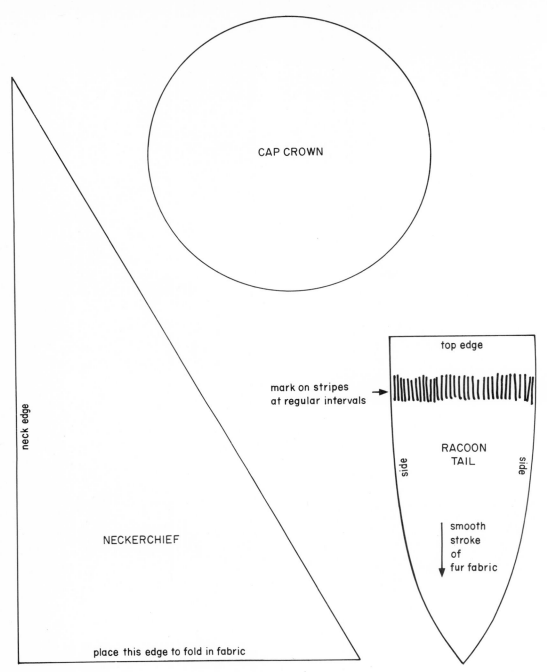

CAP CROWN

neck edge

NECKERCHIEF

place this edge to fold in fabric

top edge

mark on stripes
at regular intervals

RACOON
TAIL

side

side

smooth
stroke
of
fur fabric

Cap For the side piece cut a 5 cm by 26 cm (2in by 10¼ in) strip. Oversew the short edges together. Turn in one long edge 5 mm (¼ in) and slip stitch, for the lower edge of the cap. Run a gathering thread round the remaining raw edge.

Cut the cap crown piece and oversew the edge of this to the raw edge of the side piece, pulling up the gathers to fit.

Cut the racoon tail and mark on the stripes with marker pen as shown on the pattern. Oversew the side edges together having the right side outside, then sew the top edge to the lower edge of the cap. Place the cap on the doll's head and sew the lower edge in place.

Bend the arms and sew the hands to the belt as shown.

64

Santa Claus

MATERIALS REQUIRED

Upper body and sleeves — on Santa Claus this will
be the coat; use red felt for all the pieces including
the collar and skirt portion of the coat, plus white
fur fabric for the trimmings

Lower body — red felt

Base — cover with felt to match the feet

Feet — black felt and white fur fabric

Nose — red felt

Cap — red felt, white fur fabric and a small bell

Beard — cotton wool

Belt — grey felt and a buckle

Parcel — a matchbox, wrapping paper and ribbon

TO MAKE

Basic doll Make the basic doll using the fabrics
mentioned, but not the feet. Omit the hair since the
cap will cover the head.

For the leg portion of the boots cut a 5 cm by
26 cm (2 in by 10¼ in) strip of felt to match the
feet. Oversew the short edges of the strip together.
Put the piece on the doll's legs having the seam at

the centre back and one long edge even with the base.
Oversew the lower edge to the base. Now stitch
through the leg portion of the boots at the centre
of the legs in the same way as when dividing the legs
on the basic doll.

Make the feet as for the basic doll using the Santa
Claus foot pattern. Sew the feet in place having them
touching each other at the centre front.

Cut the nose from felt and stick it in place
between the eyes. For all the fur trimmings on the
coat and boots cut 2 cm (¾ in) wide strips of fur
fabric. Turn in the long edges of the strips to meet
each other and stick down, having the right side
outside. Stick trimming round the tops of the boots
and wrists.

Cut out the skirt portion of the coat, Stick the
trimming round the lower and front edges, then sew
the upper edge round the doll's waist.

Collar Cut out the collar. Gather the neck edge to
fit round the neck, then stick trimming to the other
edges. Place the collar in position on the doll and
catch points A together at the front of the doll.

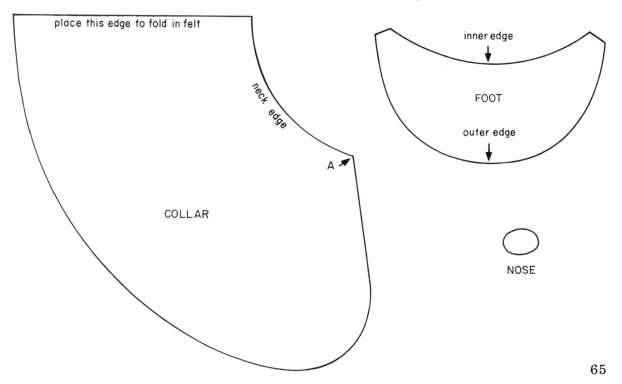

place this edge to fold in felt

neck edge

A

COLLAR

inner edge

FOOT

outer edge

NOSE

Belt Cut a strip of felt wide enough to suit the centre bar of the buckle by 30 cm (12 in) in length. Sew one end to the buckle and cut the other end to a V-shape. Place the belt on the doll and fasten at the front.

Cap Cut two cap pieces and join them, leaving the lower edges open. Trim the seam and then turn right side out. Gather round the lower edge. Place the cap on the doll's head close to the neck at the back and 2 cm (¾ in) above the eyes at the front. Pull up the gathers and fasten off, then sew the cap to the head. Sew the bell on the top point. Stick fur trimming round the lower edge and fold the top of the cap over to one side.

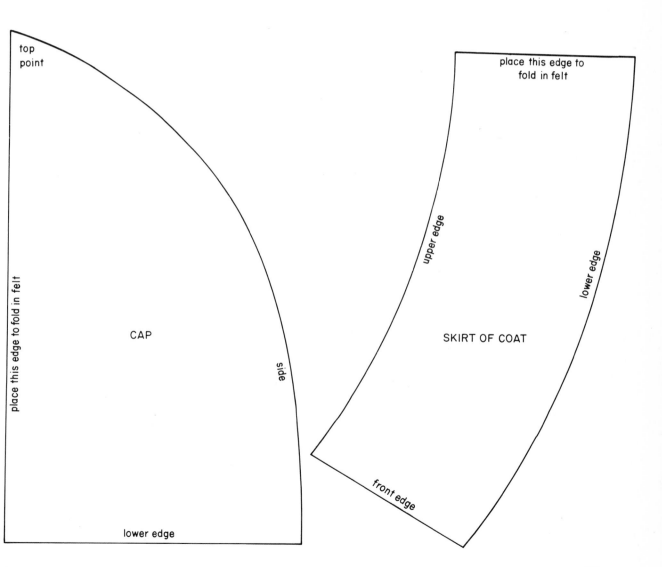

top point

place this edge to fold in felt

CAP

side

lower edge

place this edge to fold in felt

upper edge

lower edge

SKIRT OF COAT

front edge

Beard   Take a small piece of cotton wool and gently pull it to the shape of the beard pattern. Stick the beard across the face below the nose. Roll a little cotton wool between the palms of the hands, twist it at the centre and then glue this centre below the nose for the mustache. Roll up tiny pieces of cotton wool for the eyebrows and glue them in place.

Parcel   Wrap the matchbox in paper, parcel-fashion. Bend one arm around the parcel as illustrated and stick in place.

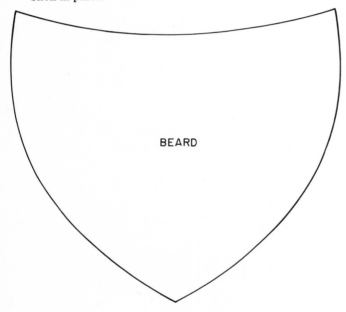

BEARD

Frankie Fascination the Pop Star

MATERIALS REQUIRED

Upper body and sleeves — plain fabric
Lower body — to match upper body
Base — cover with felt to match the lower body
Feet — felt
Mouth — red felt
Hair — long pile black fur fabric
Collar — to match the upper body
Scarf — plain silky fabric
Suit trimmings — sequined braid, fringe, or any other glittery trimmings as desired
Microphone — 2 cm (¾ in) diameter wooden macrame bead or any other bead with a large diameter hole, 4 cm (1½ in) length of thin wooden dowel to fit into the bead, silver paper, glittery fabric and length of thin cord

TO MAKE

Basic doll   Make the basic doll using the fabrics mentioned, except for the face and hair. If fringe trimming is to be added to the arms as in the doll illustrated, sew this into the sleeve seams when making up. Sew the arms to the body having the thumbs pointing away from the body.

Cut the eyelids from pink felt, then glue pieces of black felt to the lower edges as shown on the pattern. Snip the black felt into eyelashes as shown by the dotted lines. Cut the mouth from red felt and colour the centre with black marker pen. Glue the facial features in place sticking the eyelids in place but leaving the lashes free.

Cut the front and back hair pieces from fur fabric. On the back piece oversew the centre back edges together. Now join the front to the back oversewing along the top edges. Turn right side out and put the hair on the doll's head. Sew to the head round the edges. Trim the fur pile to an even length all round the lower edges.

Sew trimming down each side of the trousers, round the edges of the feet and round the lower edges of the trousers, taking it over the feet at the front.

Sew trimmings to the wrists, the chest and round the waist, referring to the illustration for ideas.

Scarf   Cut an 8 cm by 24 cm (3 in by 9½ in) strip of fabric. Fray out all the edges a little. Fold in the two long edges to meet each other, then fold the scarf in half along the length. Tie round the doll's neck as illustrated.

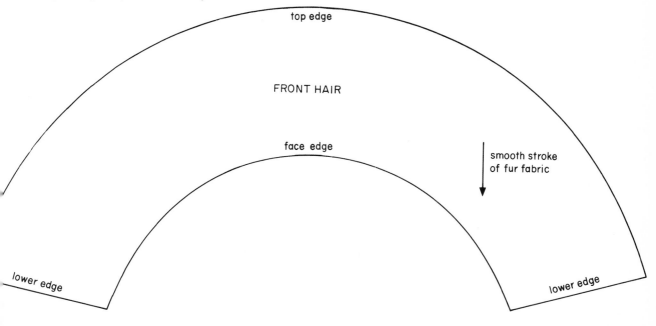

69

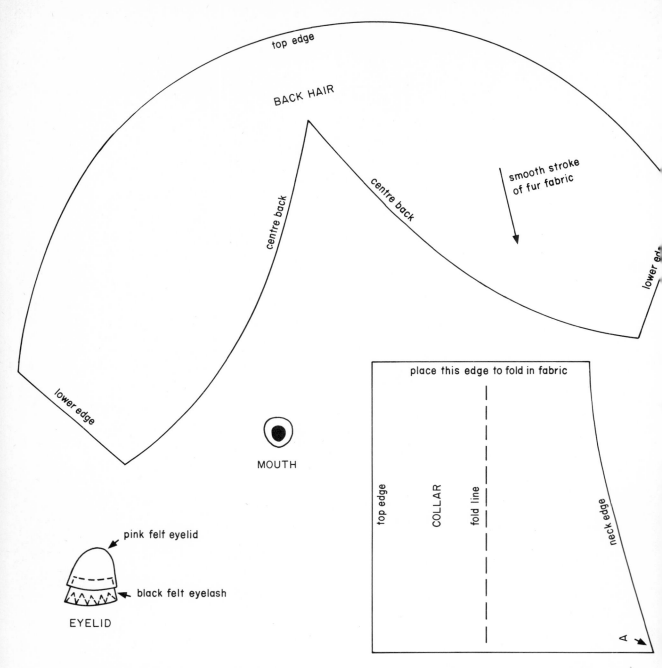

Collar Cut two collar pieces and join them round the edges leaving a gap in the neck edge for turning. Trim the seam, turn right side out and press. Slip stitch the gap. Fold the collar along the fold line and press. Place round the doll's neck and sew points A to the chest just underneath the scarf as illustrated.

Microphone Gather a piece of fabric up tightly round the bead, tying the gathers in place with thread alongside the hole in the bead. Trim the fabric close

to the tied thread, then push the raw edges of the fabric into the hole. Stick silver paper round the length of dowel and then glue one end of the dowel into the hole in the bead.

Sew one end of the cord to the palm of the doll's hand; then sew the microphone to the hand taking stitches round the dowel and into the hand.

Bend the arms at the elbows as illustrated and sew the folds in place.

70

Jolly Jack the Pirate

MATERIALS REQUIRED

Upper body and sleeves — striped fabric
Lower body — plain fabric
Base — cover with felt to match the feet
Feet — felt
Belt — leather cloth or felt and a buckle
Eye patch — felt and thin cord
Neck scarf — plain fabric
Head scarf — spotted fabric
Earring — small gold jump ring

TO MAKE

Basic doll Make the basic doll using the fabrics mentioned, except for the feet. For the hair sew a looped fringe of yarn above the eyes from one side of the head to the other.

For the leg portion of the boots cut an 8 cm by 26 cm (3¼ in by 10¼ in) strip of felt to match the feet. Oversew the short edges together. Pull one long edge of the felt to stretch it for the turned over tops of the boots. Put the piece on the doll's legs having the seam at the back and the unflared edge even with the base. Oversew the lower edge to the base.

Turn down 2 cm (¾ in) at the top, then stitch through the leg portion of the boots at the centre of the legs in the same way as when dividing the legs on the basic doll.

Make the feet as for the basic doll using the pirate foot pattern. Sew them in place having them touching each other at the centre front.

Eye patch
Cut the patch from felt and sew the top edge to the centre of a length of cord. Tie the cord round the head as illustrated, sticking the patch over one eye.

Belt Cut a strip the width of the centre bar of the buckle by 30 cm (12 in) in length. Sew one end round the buckle and cut the other end to a V-shape. Fasten the belt round the doll's waist.

Headscarf Cut a 31 cm (12¼ in) square of fabric. Fold one corner to the opposite corner and join the raw edges, taking a 3 mm ($\frac{1}{8}$ in) seam and leaving a gap for turning. Turn right side out and press, then slip stitch the gap. Tie the scarf round the doll's head knotting the narrow points at one side, then tuck in the remaining point.

Neck scarf Cut a 20 cm (8 in) square of fabric. Make as for the head scarf and then tie around the doll's neck.

Earring Sew the ring to the left side of the doll's head as illustrated. Bend the arms as illustrated and sew in place.

EYE-PATCH

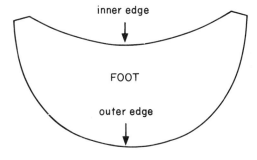

inner edge

FOOT

outer edge

Letitia Love the Tennis Player

MATERIALS REQUIRED

Upper body — white fabric
Sleeves — on the basic doll these are the bare arms, made from stockinette as given in the instructions
Lower body — flesh-coloured felt
Base — cover with felt to match the feet
Feet — white felt and narrow ribbon
Chest piece — flesh-coloured felt
Ankle socks — cutting off a man's white sock
Panties, skirt and short sleeves — white fabric and narrow white lace edging
Wrist bands — towelling fabric
Tennis racket — thin card and a piece of curtain net

TO MAKE

Basic doll   For this doll a smaller base pattern is given and also a smaller lower body piece is required. Make the basic doll except for the sleeves and feet, using the smaller base pattern and a 15 cm by 26 cm (6 in by 10¼ in) strip of flesh-coloured felt for the lower body.

Make the hands as for the basic doll, then cut two arm pieces from stockinette using the tennis player arm pattern. Join the side edges of each arm piece, then trim the seam and turn right side out. Now complete the arms and sew to the hands in exactly the same way as for the sleeves on the basic doll.

For the hair sew on strands of yarn to completely cover the head. Gather the strands to each side of the head and sew these in bunches.

For the ankle socks cut a 6 cm (2½ in) section off the leg of the sock as shown in the diagram. Place this on the doll's legs having the lower edge just above the base. Slip stitch this edge to the doll. Turn down the upper edge 1 cm (⅜ in) twice. Now stitch through the sock piece at the centre of the legs in the same way as when dividing the legs on the basic doll.

To make each knee take a tiny secure stitch 2.5 cm (1 in) above the top edge of the sock and 2 cm (¾ in) away from the centre stitching line. Pass the needle across and through the leg bringing it out 2.5 cm (1 in) away from the first stitch. Pass the needle back again and pull the thread tight to form the knee as illustrated. Fasten off the thread.

For the sides of the tennis shoes cut a 1.5 cm by 25 cm (⅝ in by 9¾ in) strip of white felt. Oversew the short edges together and then place the strip around the legs having the seam at the back. Oversew the lower edge to the edge of the base. Sew through the doll at the centre of the strip as for the socks. Make the feet as for the basic doll using the tennis player foot pattern, then sew them in place having them touching each other at the centre front. Sew small ribbon bows to the shoes as illustrated.

Chest piece   Cut the chest piece from felt and sew it to the doll in front of the neck. Sew lace edging round the edge of the chest piece and the back of the neck, forming a V-point at the front.

Panties   Cut a 6 cm by 28 cm (2½ in by 11 in) strip of white fabric. Sew lace edging to one long edge, then join the short edges. Turn right side out and put on the doll with the seam at the centre back. Gather the lace-trimmed edge to fit round the tops of the legs. Catch the lace-trimmed edge at the centre front to the centre back seam taking stitches through the doll as when dividing the legs on the basic doll. Gather the remaining raw edge and then pull up and fasten off.

Skirt   Cut a 6 cm by 45 cm (2½ in by 18 in) strip of fabric. Turn in one long edge a little and sew on lace edging. Join the short edges. Gather the remaining raw edge round the doll's waist, pull up the gathers and then fasten off. Space out the gathers evenly all round and sew to the doll.

For the waistband cut a 2.5 cm by 26 cm (1 in by 10¼ in) strip of fabric. Turn in the long edges to meet each other and press. Place around the doll's waist to cover the raw edges of the skirt, then turn in one short edge at the back and slip stitch it over the other.

Sleeves   For each sleeve cut a 4 cm by 14 cm (1½ in by 5½ in) strip of fabric. Make as for the skirt, then turn in the untrimmed raw edges a little and gather round the tops of the doll's arms. Sew the gathered edges to the body.

Wrist bands   For each one cut a 2.5 cm by 8 cm (1 in by 3 in) strip of towelling. Turn in the long

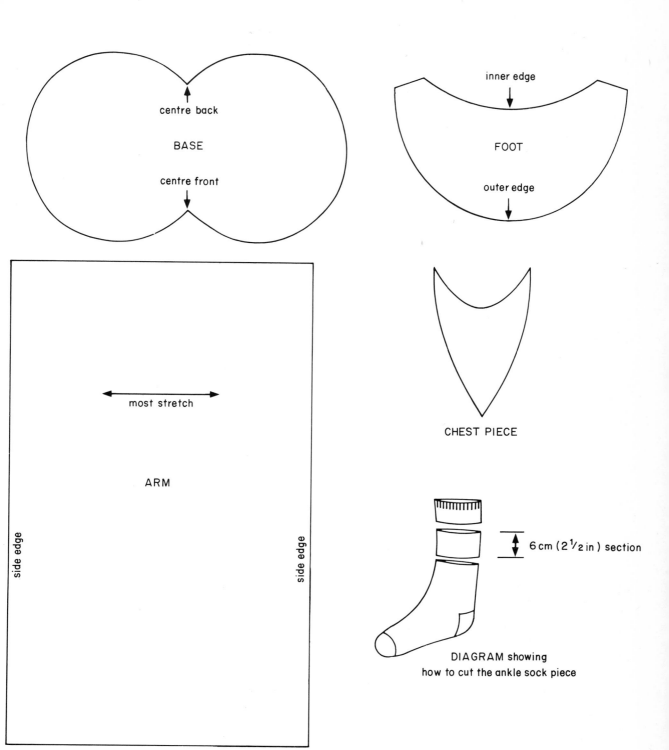

centre back

BASE

centre front

inner edge

FOOT

outer edge

CHEST PIECE

most stretch

ARM

side edge

side edge

6 cm (2½ in) section

DIAGRAM showing
how to cut the ankle sock piece

75

edges to meet each other and oversew them together. Place a wrist band round each wrist and oversew the short edges together.

Tennis racket   Trace the racket pattern off the page onto a folded piece of thin paper placing the fold along the line indicated on the pattern. Cut out, then open up and stick the paper pattern to a piece of thin card. Cut out the card even with the paper shape. Place the handle portion along the length of a pencil and bend the card against the pencil to give it a rounded effect. Colour the racket on the card side and stick on pieces of coloured paper at the positions of the shading on the pattern.

Cut a piece of curtain net to fit the racket making it a little smaller all round than the card. Stick it to the paper pattern side of the racket. Now make another card piece in the same way as the first, then stick the paper pattern sides of the two pieces together forming the complete racket.

Sew the racket to the doll's hand taking the stitches round the handle and into the hand. Bend the doll's other arm and sew the fold in place.

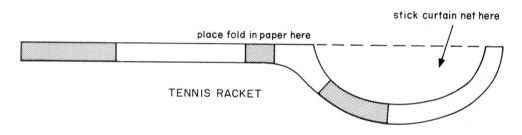

stick curtain net here

place fold in paper here

TENNIS RACKET

The Red Avenger Space Hero

MATERIALS REQUIRED

Upper body and sleeves — plain fabric
Lower body — to match the upper body
Base — cover with felt to match the feet
Feet — stretchy lurex fabric and lurex braid
Belt, collar and cuffs — stiff interlining, lurex fabric,
    lurex braid and sequins
Helmet — fabric to match the feet, narrow braid,
    and one table tennis ball
Mask — felt

TO MAKE

Basic doll   Make the basic doll using the fabrics mentioned but do not make the feet. Omit the hair since the head will be covered by the helmet.

For the leg portion of the boots, cut a 7 cm by 28 cm (2¾ in by 11 in) strip of fabric to match the feet. Join the short ends of the strip and turn in and tack the long edges. Sew the strip in place having one edge even with the base and the seam at the back. Now stitch through the leg portion of the boots at the centre in the same way as when dividing the legs on the basic doll.

Cut four foot pieces using the space hero foot pattern. Join the pieces in pairs round the outer edges taking 3 mm ($\frac{1}{8}$ in) seams. Turn right side out then turn in the remaining raw edges 3 mm ($\frac{1}{8}$ in) and tack. Stuff the feet and sew in place as for the basic doll, having them touching each other at the centre front. Sew braid round the upper edges of the leg portion of the boots.

Belt   Cut the belt from interlining and stick it onto a piece of fabric. Cut out the fabric 1 cm ($\frac{3}{8}$ in) larger all round than the interlining. Clip the extra fabric at the curves, then turn and stick it to the other side of the interlining. Stick braid to the upper and lower edges of the belt and sequins to the front, as illustrated. Place the belt around the doll's waist and sew the centre back edges together.

Cuffs   Cut the cuffs from interlining then make them as given for the belt omitting the sequins. Place one around each wrist and catch the short edges together.

Collar   Cut the collar from interlining and make

as given for the belt. Place it on the doll and catch points A together at the back. Sew the front point of the collar to the top point of the belt at the front, then catch point A to the doll's body at the back.

Mask   Cut the mask from paper, then glue this paper pattern to a piece of felt. Cut out the felt even with the paper pattern. Place the mask in position on the doll as illustrated, then sew the upper curved edge to the doll.

Helmet   Cut the helmet from fabric. Turn in the face edge 5 mm (¼ in) and catch down with small running stitches. Turn in the outer edge as for the face edge and run round a strong gathering thread. Place the helmet on the doll's head having the face edge lapping the upper edge of the mask as illustrated. Pull up the gathering thread tightly round the neck and sew points A together under the doll's chin. Sew narrow braid round the face edge.

For the ear pieces, cut the table tennis ball in half along the seam line. Stick a piece of stretchy lurex fabric to each half pulling the fabric to fit smoothly over it. Trim off the fabric 3 mm ($\frac{1}{8}$ in) away from the cut edge of each half ball. Turn this fabric to the inside and stick down. Sew or glue the ear pieces in place as illustrated.

Now sew a length of braid round the helmet above the ear pieces as illustrated. Finally place a strip of braid round the doll's neck and catch the ends together at the back.

Bend the arms and catch the hands to the belt at each side.

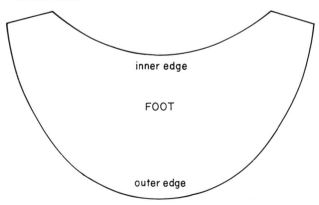

79

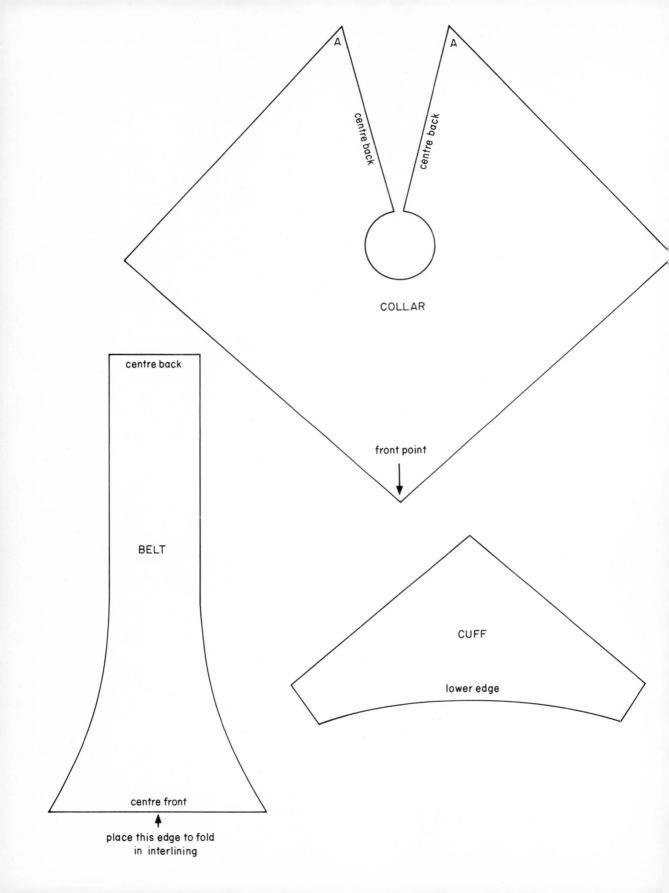

centre back

centre back

centre back

COLLAR

front point

BELT

CUFF

lower edge

centre front

place this edge to fold
in interlining

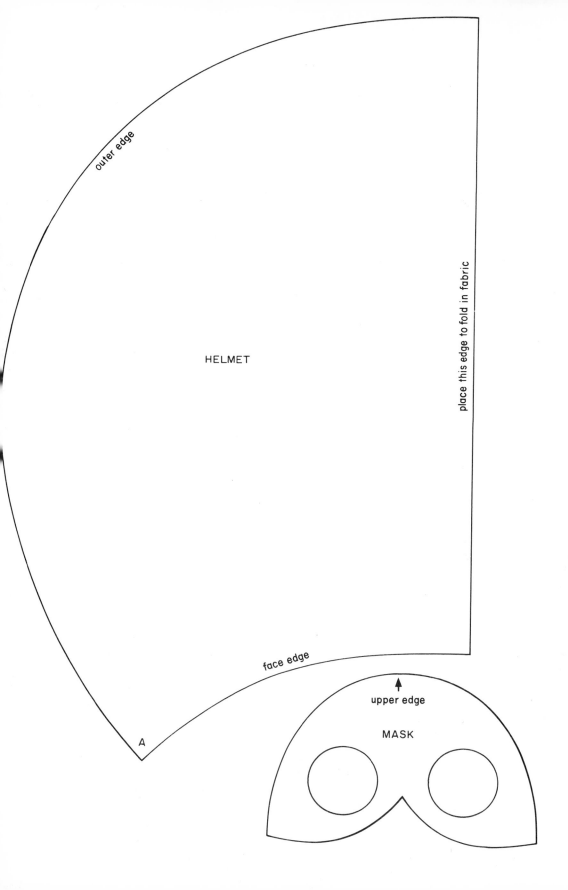

outer edge

HELMET

place this edge to fold in fabric

face edge

A

upper edge

MASK

81

Monsieur Chou-Fleur the Chef

MATERIALS REQUIRED

Upper body and sleeves — white fabric and six small white buttons

Lower body — blue and white checked fabric

Base — cover with felt to match the lower body

Feet — black felt

Mustache and eyebrows — felt to match the hair

Apron — white fabric and narrow white tape for the waistband

Cap — white fabric and stiff interlining for the cap band

Neckcloth — white fabric

Kitchen cloth — white fabric

Spoon — a salt spoon or small plastic spoon

TO MAKE

Basic doll   Make the basic doll using the fabrics mentioned. For the hair sew on a single looped fringe round the back of the head omitting the section above the eyes. For the mustache glue two layers of felt together, then cut out and glue in place as illustrated. Cut the eyebrows from felt and glue in place.

Sew the buttons to the front of the upper body as illustrated and make cuffs on the sleeves.

Apron   Cut a 10 cm by 30 cm (4 in by 12 in) strip of fabric. Make narrow hems on all the edges except for one long edge. Gather this raw edge evenly to measure 25 cm (10 in). Cut a 70 cm (28 in) length of tape and lap and stick the centre portion of the tape over the gathered edge of the apron. Place the apron around the doll, then cross over the tapes at the back and tie in a bow at the centre front. Tuck one lower corner of the apron into the waistband at one side.

Kitchen cloth   Cut a 10 cm (4 in) square of fabric. Make narrow hems on all the edges and then fold the cloth and tuck it into the waistband as illustrated.

Cap   For the cap band cut a 10 cm by 28 cm (4 in by 11 in) strip of fabric and a 4 cm by 28 cm (1½ in by 11 in) strip of interlining. Fold the fabric strip, bringing the long edges together, and press. Slip the interlining strip between the folded fabric right up against the fold. Now join the short edges of the cap band.

For the top of the cap cut a 22 cm (8¾ in) diameter circle of fabric. Run a gathering thread round the edge and pull up the gathers to fit the raw edge of the cap band, spacing out the gathers evenly. Join the cap top to the band then turn the cap right side out. Stuff the top of the cap lightly, then place on the doll's head to cover the top edges of the hair. Catch the cap to the head at the sides and back.

Neck cloth   Cut two neck cloth pieces and join them round the edges leaving a gap for turning. Trim the seams and corners, then turn right side out and press. Slip stitch the gap. Tie the cloth round the doll's neck as illustrated.

Spoon   Bend the doll's arms and catch the folds in place. Sew the spoon to one hand taking the stitches round the handle of the spoon and into the hand.

place this edge to fold in fabric

NECK CLOTH

neck edge

MUSTACHE

EYEBROW

Cowboy Joe and Miss Martha
the Cowboy and Girl
Cowboy Joe

MATERIALS REQUIRED

Upper body and sleeves — checked fabric and three
  small buttons
Lower body — white fur fabric
Base — cover with felt to match the lower body
Feet — felt
Waistcoat — felt
Belt — felt and small buckle
Neckerchief — plain or patterned fabric
Hat — felt and narrow braid

TO MAKE

Basic doll   Make the basic doll using the fabrics
mentioned. For the hair sew on a single looped
fringe. Sew the buttons down the front of the shirt
and make cuffs on the sleeves.

Belt   Cut a strip of felt the width of the centre
bar of the buckle by 30 cm (12 in) in length. Sew
one end to the buckle and cut the other end to a
V-shape. Put the belt around the waist and fasten
it at the front.

Hat   Cut two hat brim pieces. Stitch them together
all round 3 mm ($\frac{1}{8}$ in) from the outer edges. Cut
two hat crown pieces and join them taking a 5 mm
(¼ in) seam and leaving the lower edges open. Trim
the seam and turn the crown right side out. Place
the lower edge of the crown against the inner edges
of the brim and oversew the edges together. Put a
little stuffing in the crown of the hat and place it on
the doll's head, lapping it over the top edges of the
hair loops. Sew the hat to the head all round through
the base of the crown.

To indent the crown of the hat, use a long needle
to take a stitch from the back of the neck underneath the hair loops, through the head to the top
of the crown. Take the needle back again through
to the neck, pull the thread tightly, then fasten off.

Glue braid round the crown at the lower edge.
Turn up the hat brim at the front and back and
catch it to the crown with a few stitches.

Waistcoat   Cut one back piece, one pair of fronts
and two pockets using the dotted line shown on the

front pattern for the pockets. Sew the pockets in
position on the fronts. Oversew the fronts to the
back at the side and shoulder edges. Turn the waistcoat right side out, then stitch all round close to the
edges.

Neckerchief   Cut two pieces, and join them taking
a 5 mm (¼ in) seam and leaving a gap for turning.
Trim the corners, then turn right side out and slip
stitch the gap. Tie the neckerchief round the doll's
neck as illustrated.

Bend the arms and sew the hands to the doll at
each side as illustrated.

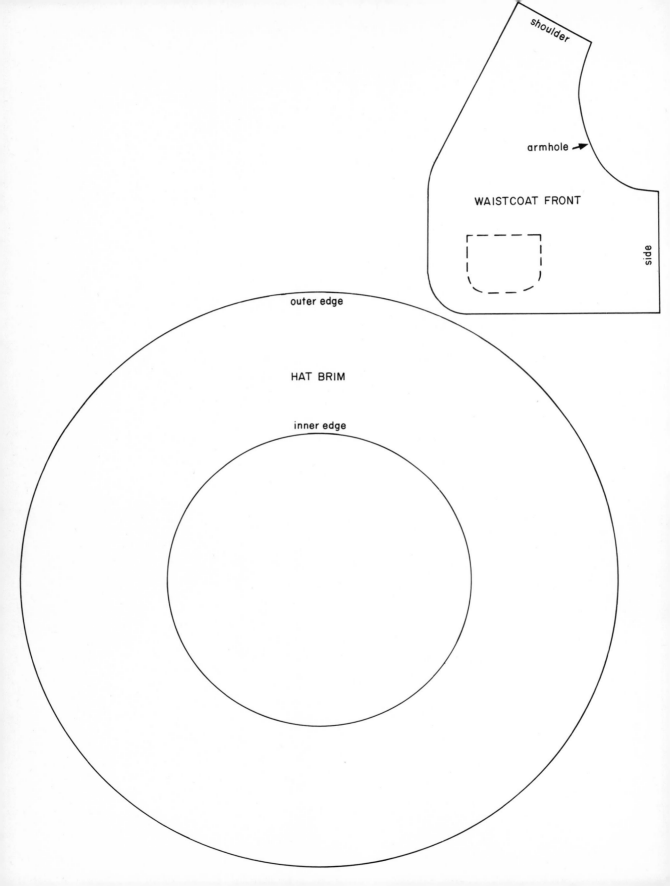

shoulder

armhole →

WAISTCOAT FRONT

side

outer edge

HAT BRIM

inner edge

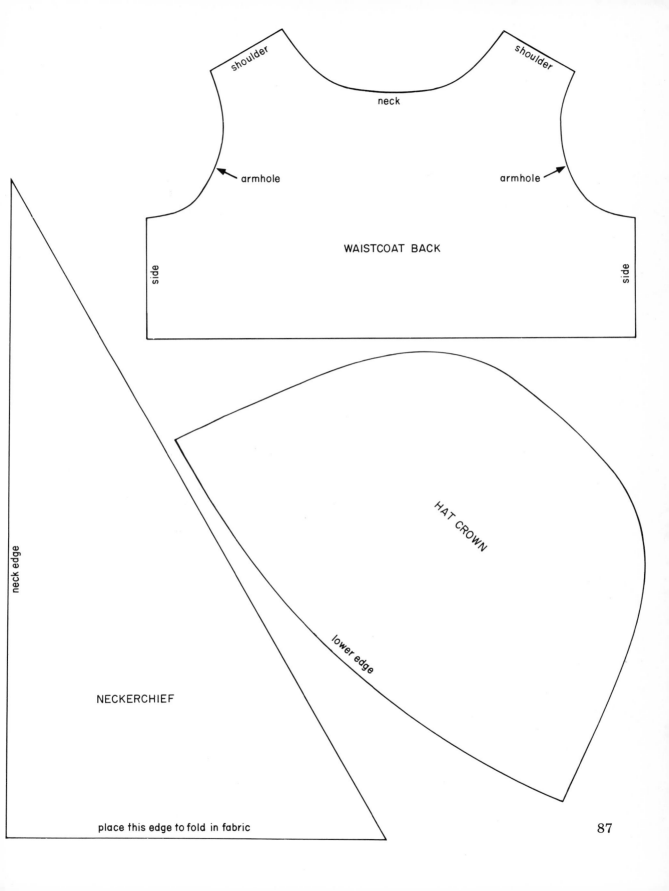

shoulder

neck

shoulder

armhole

armhole

WAISTCOAT BACK

side

side

HAT CROWN

neck edge

lower edge

NECKERCHIEF

place this edge to fold in fabric

87

Miss Martha

MATERIALS REQUIRED

Upper body and sleeves — patterned fabric, trimming and lace edging

Lower body — white fabric and lace edging

Base — cover with felt to match the lower body

Feet — felt

Skirt — as for the upper body

Apron — small checked or plain fabric and lace edging

Bonnet — plain fabric, interlining and trimming

TO MAKE

Basic doll   Make the basic doll using the fabrics mentioned. Sew on lengths of yarn at the front of the head only. Plait the yarn strands at each side, then tie a ribbon bow round the end of each plait.

Dress   For the dress skirt cut a 16 cm by 60 cm (6¼ in by 24 in) strip of fabric. Make a narrow hem along one long edge, then sew on the trimming. Join the short edges of the skirt. Gather the remaining raw edge, put the skirt on the doll then pull up the gathers to fit the waist and fasten off. Make sure that the skirt almost touches the ground, then space out the gathers evenly and sew to the doll. Sew trimming round the waist edges of the sleeves to match the skirt. For the dress collar, gather a 25 cm (10 in) length of lace edging round the neck.

Apron   Cut an 11 cm by 15 cm (4¼ in by 6 in) piece of fabric. Narrowly hem all the edges and sew on lace trimming except for one 15 cm (6 in) edge. Gather this edge to measure 8 cm (3 in). For the waistband cut a 4 cm by 50 cm (1½ in by 20 in) strip of fabric. Bind the raw edge of the apron with the centre portion of this strip, taking 5 mm (¼ in) seams. Turn in all the remaining raw edges of the strip 5 mm (¼ in) and press. Fold the strip in half along the length and stitch round the edges. Tie the apron round the doll to cover the raw edges of the skirt.

Bonnet   Cut out the bonnet crown. Run a gathering thread along the neck edge as shown on the pattern

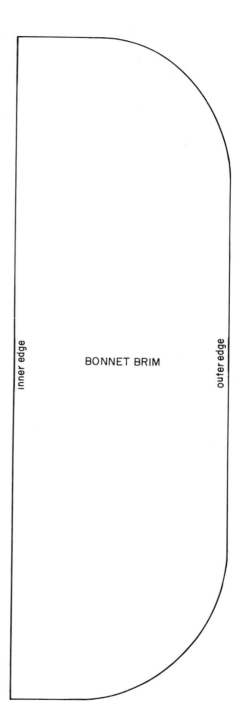

inner edge

BONNET BRIM

outer edge

and pull up the gathers until the entire neck edge measures 14 cm (5½ in). For the back neck frill cut a 5 cm by 20 cm (2 in by 8 in) strip of fabric. Take narrow hems on all the edges except for one long edge. Gather this edge to measure 13 cm (5 in). Sew this edge to the 14 cm (5½ in) edge of the bonnet between the 5 mm (¼ in) extra at each end. Gather the top edge of the bonnet crown to measure 17 cm (6¾ in).

Cut two bonnet brim pieces from fabric and one from interlining. Place the interlining on top of the fabric pieces, then join them round the outer edges taking a 5 mm (¼ in) seam. Trim the seam, turn the brim right side out and press. Stitch through the brim round the outer edge. Now join the inner raw edges of the brim to the gathered top edge of the bonnet crown taking a 5 mm (¼ in) seam.

Put a little stuffing in the gathered top of the

bonnet, then put the bonnet on the doll's head turning the raw edges of the brim to the inside. Catch the bonnet to the head at each side of the neck edge. Stick trimming to the bonnet brim where it meets the crown.

Bend the arms and sew across the folds to hold in place. Sew the right hand to the skirt as illustrated.

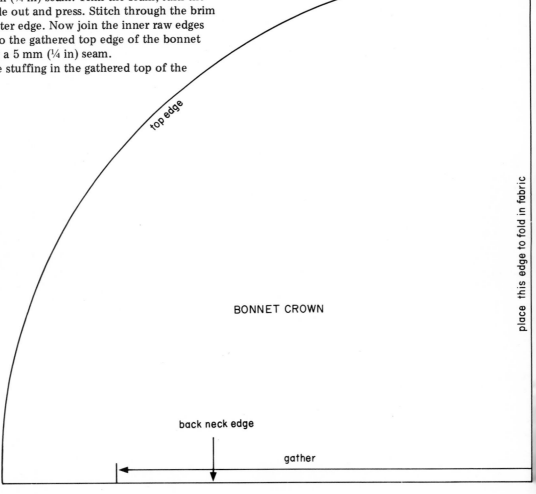

top edge

place this edge to fold in fabric

BONNET CROWN

back neck edge

gather

Madame Clara
the Gypsy Fortune Teller

MATERIALS REQUIRED

Upper body and sleeves — plain fabric
Lower body — white fabric and lace edging
Base — cover with felt to match the lower body
Feet — felt
Bead necklace — a few glass beads
Skirt — plain fabric and two contrasting colours
of ricrac braid
Bodice — felt, narrow fancy braid and thick thread
Shawl — plain fabric and braid
Head scarf — patterned fabric
Bracelets and earrings — brass curtain rings or macrame
rings, 3 cm (1¼ in) and 2 cm (¾ in) in diameter
Table — thin card, velvet and fringed trimming
Crystal ball — a large glass marble and a button
with a recessed surface to rest the marble in

TO MAKE

Basic doll Make the basic doll using the fabrics
mentioned. Omit the fringe and sew lengths of yarn
to the front of the head only. Catch the strands to
each side of the head, then sew them all together at
the back of the head above the neck and trim the
ends evenly.

Bead necklace Thread the beads and tie them round
the doll's neck as illustrated.

Skirt Cut an 11 cm by 50 cm (4¼ in by 20 in)
strip of fabric. Sew the ricrac braid to the skirt
1 cm (⅜ in) away from one long raw edge. Join the
short edges of the skirt. For the frill cut a 6 cm by
90 cm (2¼ in by 36 in) strip of fabric. Join the
short edges then make a narrow hem on one long
edge. Gather the remaining raw edge to fit the ricrac
trimming edge of the skirt and then sew it in place.

Gather the remaining raw edge of the skirt around
the doll's waist, pull up the gathers and fasten off.
Sew the raw edge to the doll spacing out the gathers
evenly all round.

Bodice Cut out the bodice back and one pair of
fronts. Join the fronts to the back at the sides and
shoulders oversewing the edges together. Now sew
braid round the armhole and outer edges. Place the
bodice on the doll and use a needle and thread to
lace the front edges together as illustrated. Tie the
thread ends in a bow at the top.

Shawl Cut a 32 cm (12½ in) square of fabric.
Take a narrow hem round the edges and then sew
on the trimming. Fold into a triangle and then drape
the shawl around the doll, catching it to the arms
as illustrated.

Head scarf Make as for the shawl, omitting the
trimming, then tie around the doll's head knotting
the points at one side Sew the scarf to the head.

Bracelets and earrings Push the largest rings over
the doll's hands and onto the wrists. Sew the smaller
rings to the head at each side as illustrated.

Table Cut an 11 cm by 32 cm (4¼ in by 12½ in)
strip of card. Bend it into a tube-shape lapping and
sticking 2 cm (¾ in) at the short ends. At one end of
the tube glue on a 10 cm (4 in) diameter circle of
card for the the table top.

For the table cloth cut a 32 cm (12½ in) diameter
circle of velvet. Sew fringe round the circle, having
the lower edge of the fringe even with the edge of
the circle and easing the fringe round the curve.
Place the cloth over the table and stick it in folds
here and there to the card.

Bend the arms and sew across the folds to hold
in place.

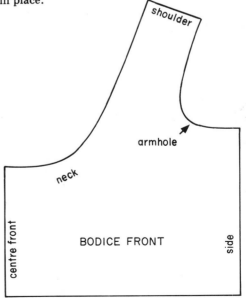

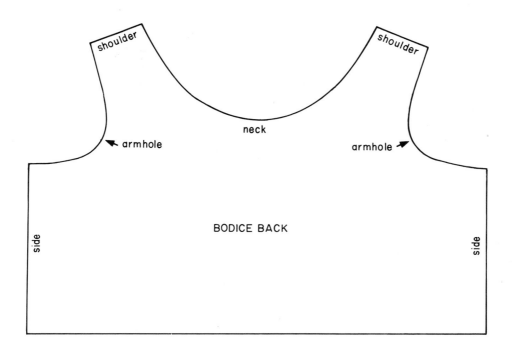

BODICE BACK

Sylvia Sparkle *the Skier*

MATERIALS REQUIRED

Upper body and sleeves — plain fabric and narrow
    striped or plain ribbon
Lower body — to match the upper body
Base — cover with felt to match the lower body
Feet — felt
Ski boot fastenings — felt
Collar — to match the upper body
Hands, ski hat and polo collar — one ankle or knee
    sock and guipure flower trimming or braid
Skis — thin card and coloured paper
Glasses — coloured acetate film

TO MAKE

Basic doll   Cut the lower body and sleeves as for the
basic doll, then sew the ribbon to the position of the
'side seams' on the lower body piece and sew ribbon
up the centre of the sleeve pieces as well. Now make
the basic doll using the fabrics mentioned but do not
make the hands, sleeves or feet.

For the hair omit the fringe and sew on lengths
of yarn at the front of the head only. Catch the
strands to each side of the head, then trim the ends
of the yarn evenly. Sew ribbon to the centre front
of the upper body as illustrated.

Sew the sleeves as for the basic doll and turn right
side out. Run a gathering thread round one end of
each sleeve, pull up tightly and fasten off. Stuff the
sleeves and finish the top edges as for the basic doll.
Sew the hands as for the basic doll using pieces cut
off the leg of the sock. Turn and stuff the hands,
then turn in the wrist edges and slip these over the
gathered edges of the sleeves. Slip stitch the hands
to the arms, taking care to position one hand so that
the thumb will point away from the body when the
arms are sewn in place. This hand will hold the skis.
Sew trimming or braid to the hands, then sew the
arms to the body.

Cut two lower and two upper foot pieces from
felt using the skier patterns. On the upper pieces
oversew the edges of the darts together. Now make
the feet and sew in place as for the basic doll, having
them touching each other at the centre front.

Ski boot fastenings   Cut these from felt as shown on
the pattern. Glue the smaller felt pieces to the larger

pieces and then stick them in place on the boots
as illustrated.

Polo collar   Cut a 4 cm by 8 cm (1½ in by 3 in)
strip off the leg of the sock. Roll down one long
edge, then place around the doll's neck and join the
short edges at the back.

Collar   Cut a 5 cm by 15 cm (2 in by 6 in) strip of
fabric. Fold in half bringing the long edges together.
Join round the raw edges, leaving a gap for turning.
Trim the seam, turn right side out and slip stitch the
gap, then press. Place the collar round the doll's
neck and catch the lower corners to the doll at the
front as illustrated.

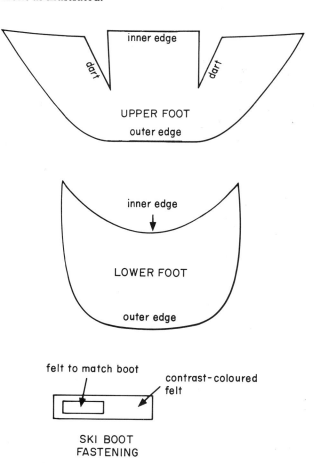

Glasses Cut the glasses from acetate film and place on the doll slipping the arm pieces of the glasses through the doll's hair. Stick these to the head at each side.

Ski cap The foot portion of the sock is used for the cap. Measure and cut an 18 cm (7 in) length from the toe end of the sock. Turn back the cut edge 3 cm (1¼ in) twice. Place the cap on the doll's head and catch it to the head at the front, back and sides. Sew on trimming or braid as illustrated.

Skis Cut two from white paper for the underside of the skis. Stick the paper pieces to thin card and cut out the card even with the paper. Curl up the front and back of each ski beyond the dotted lines. Make the upper face of each ski in the same way using coloured paper instead of white. Stick the ski pieces together, then decorate each one as shown in the illustration.

    Glue the undersides of the skis together, then stick the doll's hand around the skis as illustrated. Bend the arms and sew across the folds and then sew the free hand to the doll's side.

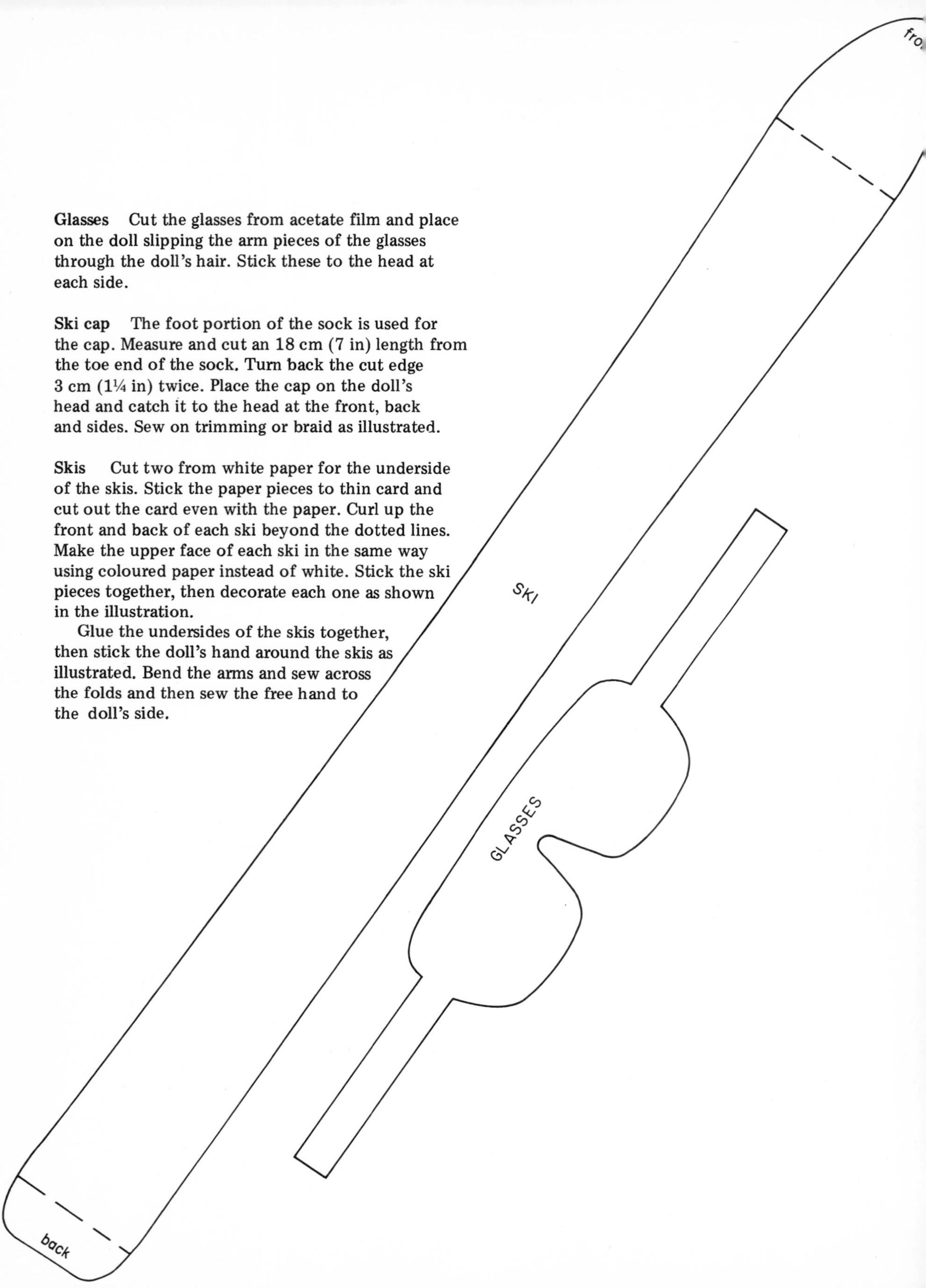

fro

SKI

GLASSES

back

Robin Hood

MATERIALS REQUIRED

Upper body and sleeves — green felt, making the
   sleeves in a darker shade than the body
Lower body — green fabric in a different shade from
   the upper body
Base — cover with felt to match the feet
Feet — fawn felt
Tunic skirt — green felt to match the upper body
   and ricrac braid
Belt — brown felt and a small buckle
Hood — green felt in a different shade from the
   other pieces and ricrac braid

TO MAKE

Basic doll   Make the doll using the fabrics
mentioned, but not the feet. For the hair sew on a
few loops of yarn above the eyes, then sew another
row of loops above this from one side of the head,
across the forehead, to the other side.

   For the leg portion of the boots cut a 7cm by
26 cm (2¾ in by 10¼ in) strip of felt to match the
feet. Oversew the short edges of the strip together.
Pull one long edge to stretch it slightly. Put the
piece on the doll with the seam at the back and
having the unstretched edge even with the base.
Sew this edge to the base. Turn down 2 cm (¾ in)
at the top, then sew through the leg portion of the
boots at the centre of the legs in the same way as
when dividing the legs on the basic doll.

Make the feet as for the basic doll using the Robin
Hood foot pattern. Sew them in place having them
touching each other at the centre front.

Tunic skirt   Cut a 5 cm by 30 cm (2 in by 12 in)
strip of felt. Sew braid to one long edge for the hem
edge. Oversew the short edges together and turn right
side out. Gather and sew the remaining edge round
the doll's waist having the seam at the back and
spacing out the gathers evenly.

Belt   Cut a strip of felt the width of the centre
bar of the buckle by 30 cm (12 in) in length. Sew
one end round the buckle and cut the other end to
a V-shape. Fasten the belt round the doll's waist.

Hood   Cut the head portion from felt. Oversew
the back edges together, then turn right side out.
Run a gathering thread round the neck edge. Cut
the cape portion from felt and pull up the gathers
in the head portion to fit the neck edge of the cape.
Oversew the neck edges together spacing out the
gathers evenly. Sew braid round the lower edge of
the cape.

   Place the hood on the doll's head and catch the
neck edges together below the chin. Fold the point
of the hood down at the back and catch it to the
back seam of the hood.

   Bend the arms and sew the hands to the doll's
body at each side, or bend one arm to rest on Friar
Tuck's shoulder as illustrated.

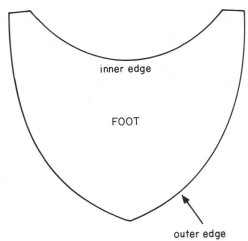

inner edge

FOOT

outer edge

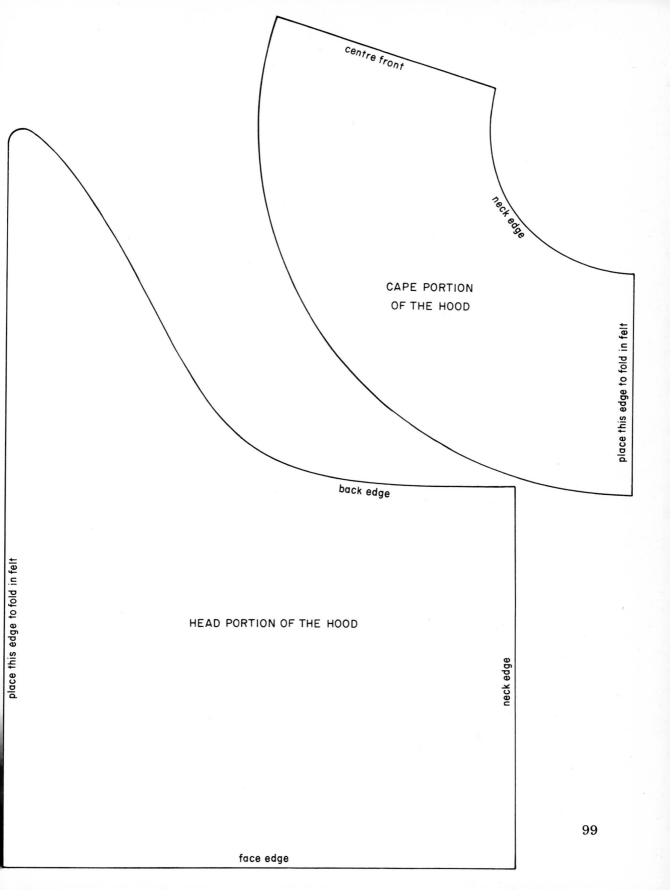

centre front

neck edge

CAPE PORTION
OF THE HOOD

place this edge to fold in felt

back edge

place this edge to fold in felt

HEAD PORTION OF THE HOOD

neck edge

99

face edge

Friar Tuck

MATERIALS REQUIRED

Upper body — brown felt
Sleeves — on the basic doll these are the bare arms
    made from stockinette as given in the instructions
Lower body — pink or cream fabric
Base — cover with brown felt to match the sandals
Feet — stockinette to match the head and hands
Tunic skirt, tunic sleeves and collar — brown felt to
    match the upper body
Sandals — brown felt
Girdle — 85 cm (34 in) length of piping cord
Stick — a 22 cm (8¾ in) length of twig or dowelling
    about 5 mm (¼ in) in diameter

TO MAKE

Basic doll   Make the basic doll using the fabrics
mentioned, but not the feet, arms and hair. Make the
hands as for the basic doll, then cut two arm pieces
from stockinette using the Friar Tuck pattern.
Join the side edges of each piece and trim the seams,
then turn right side out. Now complete the arms and
sew to the hands in exactly the same way as for the
sleeves on the basic doll. When sewing the arms in
place, position the right arm so that the thumb
points away from the body.

For the hair sew on a single looped fringe. To
cover the bald top of the head cut a 9 cm (3½ in)
and a 10 cm (4 in) diameter circle of stockinette.
Place the small circle on the doll's head with the
larger circle on top of it. Turn in the raw edge of the
top circle 5 mm (¼ in) and pin it to the head all
round the edge to cover the top loops of the hair.
Slip stitch in place as pinned.

Cut two pairs of foot pieces from stockinette,
using the bare foot pattern. Join the pieces in pairs
taking 3 mm ($\frac{1}{8}$ in) seams and leaving the inner edges
open. Trim the seams and turn right side out. Turn

in the inner edges 5 mm (¼ in) and tack loosely.
Stuff the feet lightly and sew them in place as for the
basic doll's feet. Make the toes by working four
stitches around and through each foot, as shown in
the illustration, using matching thread.

Sandals   Cut a pair of soles from brown felt and
place one under each foot; then catch the inner edge
of the soles to the edge of the base. Cut 5 mm (¼ in)
wide strips of felt for the straps and stick one strip
to each foot to pass over the big toe from the leg
to under the sole. Stick another strip across each
foot close to the leg, tucking it under the sole at
each side.

Tunic skirt   Cut a 12 cm by 32 cm (4¾ in by 12½ in)
strip of brown felt. Join the short edges oversewing
them together and then turn right side out. Gather
one long edge around the doll's waist and sew in
place, spacing out the gathers evenly.

Tunic sleeves   Cut two sleeves from brown felt.
Oversew the underarm edges together and turn right
side out. Place a sleeve on each arm and slip stitch
the armhole edges to the doll's body.

Collar   Cut the collar from brown felt. Place it in
position on the doll and oversew the centre back
edges together at the back. Gather the neck edge
and pull up the gathers to fit the neck, then fasten
off.

Girdle   Tie the piping cord round the waist as
illustrated, knotting it at the front; then knot the
ends of the cord.

Stick   Place the stick in position and sew the right
hand to it taking the stitches around the stick and
into the hand. Bend the arms and catch the folds in
place, sewing right through the sleeves and into the
arms.

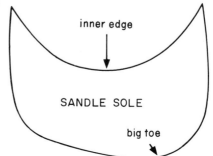

inner edge

BARE FOOT

most stretch

big toe

outer edge

SANDLE SOLE

big toe

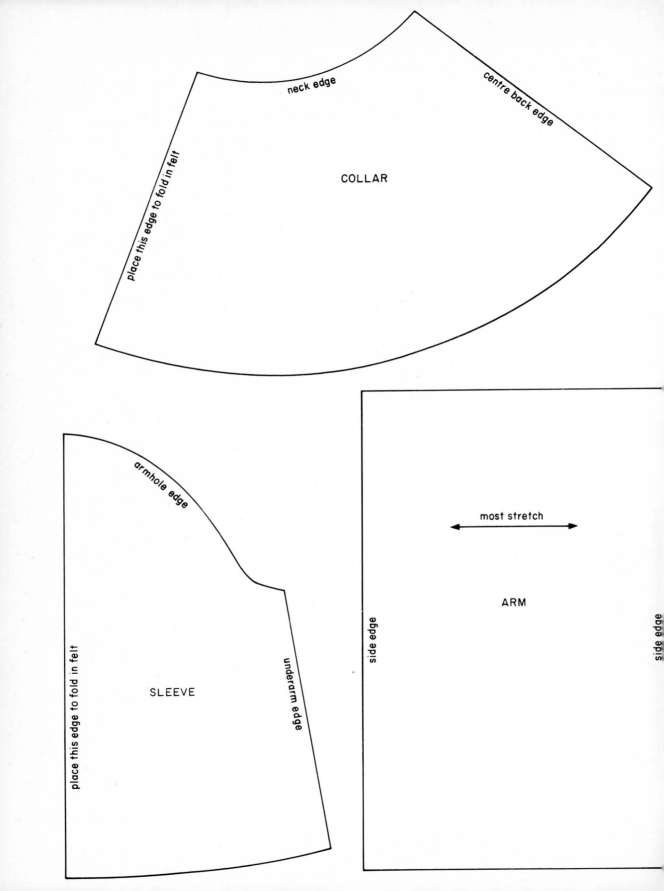

Gloria Glamor the Film Star

MATERIALS REQUIRED

Upper body and sleeves — satin, or other shiny
    fabric
Lower body — to match the upper body
Base — cover with felt to match the lower body
Feet — omit the feet since they will spoil the line
    of the dress on the finished doll
Mouth — red felt
Hem frill — to match the upper body
Sash — thin soft fabric
Fur stole — white fur fabric
Jewellery — use any pieces of diamante junk
    jewellery and beads as available; alternatively
    use sequins

TO MAKE

Basic doll   Make the basic doll using the fabrics
mentioned but do not work the stitching to divide
the body for the legs. Omit the feet as well. Sew the
left arm in place with the thumb pointing away
from the body. Work black stitches above the eyes
for the eyelashes as illustrated. Cut the mouth from
red felt and mark the centre with black pen or
pencil. Glue the mouth in place.

MOUTH

For the hair use mohair or similar yarn instead of
chunky or double knitting. Wind the yarn 30 times
around a 34 cm (13½ in) length of stiff card. Slip
this hank off the card and tie a strand of yarn round
the hank a little off centre. Sew this tied portion to
the doll's head at the position of the 'side parting'.

Take the strands to the sides of the head, then
bring the looped ends together at the back of the
head and sew them in place. Make two more hanks
of yarn in the same way, then twist each one a few
times bringing the looped ends together. Sew one of
these twisted hanks to the back of the head and one
to the top to completely cover the head.

Hem frill   Cut an 8 cm by 70 cm (3¼ in by 28 in)
strip of fabric. Join the short ends. Make a narrow
hem on one long edge. Turn in the remaining raw
edge and run round a strong gathering thread. Place
the frill on the doll and pull up the thread very
tightly, then fasten off. Space out the gathers evenly
and make sure that the hem of the frill touches
the ground. Sew the gathered edge in place.

Sash   Cut a 12 cm by 60 cm (4¾ in by 24 in)
strip of fabric. Turn in the long edges to meet each
other, then fold the sash in half along the length.
Place it round the doll's waist and knot at one side.
Sew the knot in place, form the remainder of the
sash into loops as illustrated and then sew in place.

Fur stole   Cut an 8 cm by 75 cm (3¼ in by 30 in)
strip of fur fabric. Fold in half along the length and
oversew the raw edges together all round, leaving
a gap in the long edge and rounding off the corners
at each end. Turn right side out through the gap
pushing each end through with a knitting needle.
Slip stitch the gap. Arrange the stole on the doll
as illustrated.

Jewellery   Sew pieces of jewellery, beads etc. to
the doll as illustrated. Sew the right hand to the
hip, then bend the left arm upwards and sew the
fold in place.

WG Wicket the Cricketer

MATERIALS REQUIRED

Upper body and sleeves — white fabric
Lower body — white fabric
Base — cover with felt to match the lower body
Feet — white felt
Chest piece — flesh-coloured felt
Waistband and shirt collar — white fabric
Shirt buttons — the buttons on the doll illustrated
    are cut from white card using a leather punch
    to make perfect circles; alternatively, use white
    sequins
Cricket pads — white fabric, thin wadding for padding
    and leather cloth for the straps
Cap — felt, in the desired club colour and iron-on
    interlining

TO MAKE

Basic doll   Make the basic doll using the fabrics
mentioned. Make cuffs on the shirt sleeves. For the
hair sew on a single looped fringe.

Waistband   Cut two 3 cm by 28 cm (1¼ in by
11 in) strips of fabric. Join them round the edges
leaving a gap for turning and making a V-point at
one end. Trim the seam and turn right side out using
a knitting needle to push the ends through. Slip
stitch the gap and press the band. Place round the
doll's waist, then lap the V-point over the other
end and sew in place.

Chest piece   Cut the chest piece from felt and sew
to the doll in front of the neck.

Shirt collar   Cut two collar pieces and join them
round the edges taking a 3 mm ($\frac{1}{8}$ in) seam and
leaving a gap in the top edge for turning.
    Snip off the corners, turn right side out and
press, then slip stitch the gap. Fold the collar down
at the dotted line and press. Now place the folded
collar round the doll's neck and lap the left front
straight piece over the right front straight piece as
illustrated. Sew the collar and front pieces to the
doll, then stick on the buttons as illustrated.

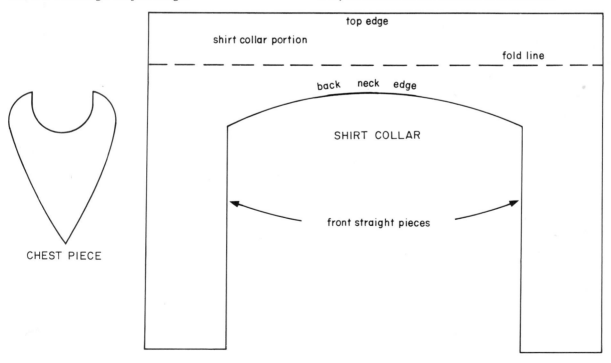

CHEST PIECE

top edge

shirt collar portion

fold line

back   neck   edge

SHIRT COLLAR

front straight pieces

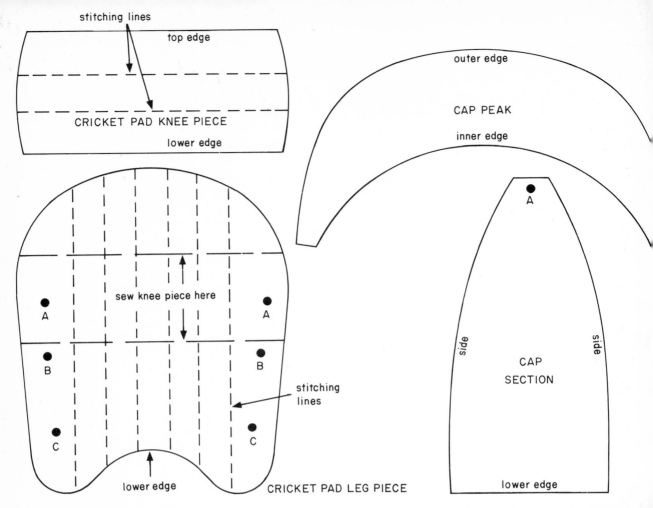

Cricket pads   Take 3 mm ($\frac{1}{8}$ in) seams on all the pieces. For each pad cut two leg pieces from fabric and one from wadding. Place the fabric pieces on top of the wadding piece. Join all the pieces leaving a gap in the lower edge. Turn right side out and slip stitch the gap. Now machine stitch along all the dotted lines indicated on the pattern.

Make the knee pieces in the same way as for the leg pieces. Sew the knee pieces in position on the leg pieces. Pin the pads to the doll's legs as illustrated. For the top strap cut a 3 mm by 15 cm ($\frac{1}{8}$ in by 6 in) strip of leather cloth and for each of the other two straps a 3 mm by 14 cm ($\frac{1}{8}$ in by 5½ in) strip. Place the top strap round the back of the doll's legs and pin each end to points A shown on the pattern on the outside of the legs. Pin the other two straps in place in the same way to points B and C. Remove the pads and sew the ends of the straps in place as pinned.

Place the pads on the legs again. Using strong thread, sew through the straps and the doll from the centre back to the pads at the front at positions A, B and C.

Cap   Take 3 mm ($\frac{1}{8}$ in) seams on all the cap pieces unless otherwise stated. Cut eight cap section pieces. Join them together in pairs at one side from the lower edges to point A. Press the seams open. Now join the pairs to form two sections of four, and finally join both sections of four at the remaining side edges. Press all seams open. Turn in the lower edge 1 cm ($\frac{3}{8}$ in) and press. Catch in place at the position of each seam.

Iron the interlining onto a piece of felt and then cut out two cap peak pieces. Join them round the outer edges, trim the seam and turn right side out. Press the peak, then oversew the inner edges together. Place the peak in position at the lower edge of the cap against three of the sections as illustrated, then sew in place. Sew the cap to the doll's head at the back and sides.

Bend the doll's arms and sew the hands to the sides.

108

Grizelda Grim
the Witch

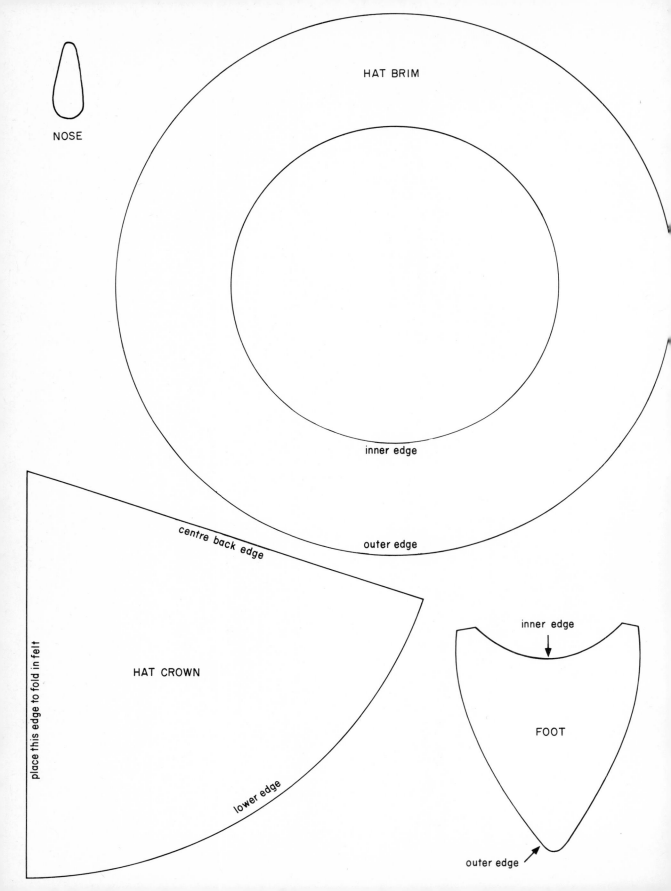

NOSE

HAT BRIM

inner edge

outer edge

centre back edge

place this edge to fold in felt

HAT CROWN

lower edge

inner edge

FOOT

outer edge

MATERIALS REQUIRED

Upper body and sleeves — plain fabric and lace edging

Lower body — plain fabric and lace edging

Base — cover with felt to match the lower body

Feet — felt

Nose — red felt

Skirt — patterned fabric, ricrac braid and tape or ribbon for the waistband

Cape — black fabric and ribbon

Hat — black felt, thin card and ricrac braid

Stick — a 15 cm (6 in) length of twig about 1 cm (¼ in) in diameter

Book of spells — matchbox and coloured paper

TO MAKE

Basic doll   Make the basic doll using the fabrics mentioned except for the face, feet and hair. Bend the doll forward and sew a small tuck across the upper body fabric close to the waist to hold the doll in this bent position. When sewing the arms in place, position them a little closer to the front than on the basic doll.

For the hair cut 6 cm (2¼ in) lengths of green yarn. Lay them side by side and machine stitch them together along one edge forming a fringe about 22 cm (8½ in) in length. Sew the hair in place just before fitting on the hat so that it is positioned as shown in the illustration. Colour the cheeks with green instead of red pencil.

Stick the eyes closer together and higher up the face than for the basic doll. Cut the nose from red felt and stick it in place as illustrated. Work black stitches above the eyes as shown in the illustration. Make the first mouth stitch as for the basic doll but place the second smaller stitch above the mouth to pull the centre of the stitch upwards.

Make the feet and sew in place as for the basic doll using the witch's foot pattern. Sew lace edging round the wrist edges of the sleeves.

Skirt   Cut a 15 cm by 42 cm (6 in by 16½ in) strip of fabric. Hem one long edge and sew on the braid. Join the short edges. Gather the remaining raw edge round the doll's waist. Pull up the gathers and sew the raw edge to the body, spacing out the gathers evenly. Place the tape or ribbon round the waist to cover the raw edge and lap and sew the ends at the back.

Hat   Cut two hat brim pieces from felt and another piece from card. Trim a little off the outer and inner edges of the card piece. Stick the felt pieces together sandwiching the card piece between them. Stitch all round close to the outer edge of the brim.

Cut the crown of the hat and oversew the centre back edges together. Turn right side out. Oversew the lower edge of the crown to the inner edge of the brim. Stuff the crown of the hat lightly. Place the hat in position on the head and then pin the hair in place, tucking it under the hat. Sew the hair in place, then catch the hat to the head all round where the crown meets the brim. Glue the braid round the hat for the hat band.

Cape   Cut a 25 cm by 32 cm (10 in by 12½ in) piece of fabric. Hem all the edges except for one 32 cm (12½ in) edge. Turn in this edge and gather, then place it round the doll's neck, pulling up the gathering stitches tightly and sewing the ends together at the front. Sew a ribbon bow to the front neck edge.

Stick   If possible, use a twig with a 'branch' at the top for a handle. Sew the handle to the doll's hand, taking the stitches around the twig and into the hand.

Book of spells   Slide out the matchbox tray and glue a strip of paper ruled into lines to resemble pages round the side of the tray. Take the slide-on cover and cut away one long narrow side and discard it. Glue coloured paper to the remainder of the slide-on cover for the cover of the book. Write the words 'MAGIC SPELLS' on the cover and then glue the cover in place around the matchbox tray.

Bend the arms as illustrated and sew across the folds. Tuck the book under one arm and fix it in place with dabs of adhesive where it touches the arm and body.

Olaf the Awful the Viking

MATERIALS REQUIRED

Upper body and sleeves — tan or orange fabric and
  narrow braid with a geometric pattern
Lower body — brown fabric
Base — cover to match the feet
Feet — chamois leather or felt
Nose — red felt
Beard, mustache and hair — fawn fur fabric
Leg bindings — narrow black elastic
Tunic — to match the upper body
Belt — brown leather cloth or felt and a small buckle
Cloak — green felt
Cloak pin — a button and gold cord
Helmet — dark grey felt, iron-on interlining and
  black braid

TO MAKE

Basic doll   Make the basic doll using the fabrics
mentioned except for the hair and feet. Do not sew
the arms to the body at this stage. Cut the nose
from felt and stick in place.

For the sides of the shoes cut a 1.5 cm by 25 cm
($\frac{5}{8}$ in by 9¾ in) strip of chamois or felt. Oversew
the short edges together, then place the strip on the
doll having the seam at the back. Oversew the lower
edge of the strip to the edge of the base. Slip stitch
the other edge to the doll and then sew through the
doll at the centre of the strip as when dividing the
legs on the basic doll. Make the feet as for the basic
doll using the Viking foot pattern. Sew them in place,
having them touching each other the centre
front.

Sew a length of elastic to the legs round the tops
of the shoes. For each leg binding cut a 70 cm (28 in)
length of elastic. Use a darning needle to take one
end of each length through the centre of the doll
from front to back just above the shoes. Bring the
other ends of the elastic through from the back of
the doll in the same way. Now continue this process,
crossing over the elastics and sewing them through
the centre of the doll until about half-way up the
legs, to give the cross-laced effect as shown in the
illustration. Finish by knotting the ends of the
elastic together at the back of each leg.

Tunic   For the body of the tunic cut a 17 cm by
32 cm (6¾ in by 12½ in) strip of fabric. turn in one
long edge, stitch it down and then sew on braid. Join
the short edges of the strip. Turn in the remaining
raw edge and run round a gathering thread. Put the
tunic on the doll having the seam at the centre
back, then pull up the gathers round the neck and
fasten off.

Now sew the arms in place as for the basic doll
taking the stitches through the tunic and into the
body. Sew braid round the wrist edges of the sleeves.

Belt   Cut a strip, the width of the centre bar of the
buckle by 30 cm (12 in) in length. Sew one end
round the centre bar and cut the other end to a
V-shape. Place the belt round the tunic and fasten
at the front.

Cloak   Cut the cloak from felt and make two pleats
in the front edges as shown on the pattern, folding
the solid lines to the dotted lines. Oversew the edges
to hold the pleats in position. Place the cloak round
the doll's neck and lap one pleated edge slightly
over the other at the front. Sew the edge in place.

Cloak pin   Glue the gold cord round and round
onto the button to cover it, then sew the button
to the pleats.

Beard   Cut the beard from fur fabric. Turn in the
top edge a tiny bit and catch down. Sew the top
edge of the beard to the face having the centre about
1.5 cm ($\frac{5}{8}$ in) below the nose.

Mustache   Cut the mustache from fur fabric and
oversew the upper and lower edges together having

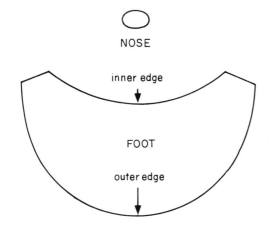

NOSE

inner edge
↓

FOOT

outer edge
↓

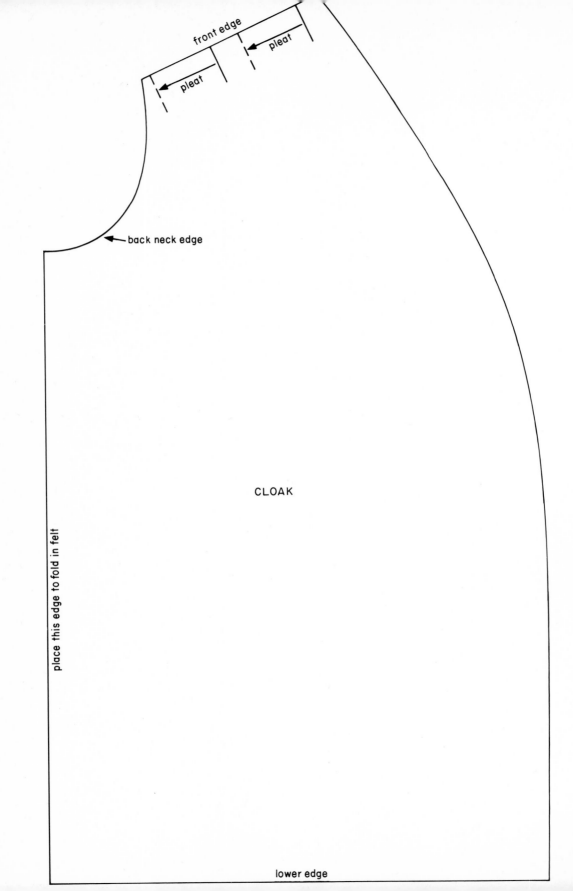

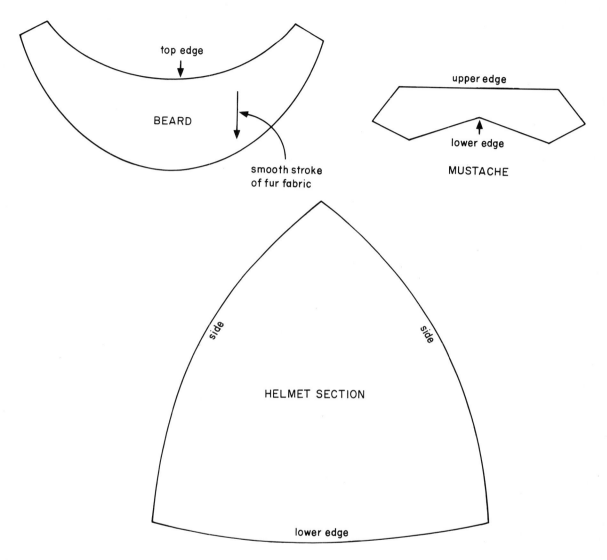

the right side outside. Keeping this seam at the back, sew the centre of the mustache in place below the nose.

Hair   Cut a 5 cm by 21 cm (2 in by 8¼ in) strip of fur fabric. Turn in the ends and slip stitch. Pin the strip around the sides and back of the head about 5 cm (2 in) down from the gathered top of the head. Sew the top edge in place as pinned.

Helmet   Iron the interlining onto the back of the felt, then cut out four helmet section pieces. Join them in pairs at one side edge. Press the seams open and then trim them. Now join the pairs at the remaining side edges, then press and trim the seams as before. Turn the helmet right side out. Stick the braid over all the helmet seams, then stick braid round the lower edge. Place the helmet on the doll's head to cover the top edge of the hair and then catch it in place at the back and sides.

Bend the arms and sew the hands to the sides as illustrated.

Suggestions for 30 more dolls

Masked cowboy (lone ranger)
As for the cowboy, making all the clothes either white or black. Make a mask from the space hero mask making the upper edge the same shape as the lower edge.

Sally scarecrow
Make ragged and patched clothes as for Cinderella with 'straw' hair, etc. as for the scarecrow.

Mrs Claus (to go with Santa Claus)
Use red and white fabrics to make suitable garments adapted from any female dolls.

Bridesmaid
Make as for the bride with a flower head dress and small bouquet.

Cinderella's ugly sisters
Make smaller and taller basic dolls by shortening and lengthening the upper and lower body pieces, the arm and head pieces by 1 cm ($\frac{3}{8}$ in) for each character.

Red Riding Hood
Make the dress and apron as for Miss Martha. Use the Robin Hood pattern to make a red hood, omitting the top point at the top of the hood. Add a tiny basket.

Doll in track suit (for jogging and other sports)
Use the skier for the basic idea.

Dolls in shorts (cycling, running, table tennis, etc.)
Adapt the footballer or tennis player to suit any sports outfit with bare legs and arms. Note that the upper body may also be made from flesh-coloured felt.

Suffragette
Simplify the Edwardian lady's costume using plain fabrics and braids for trimming instead of lace. Make a placard fixed to the end of a length of dowel and mark on the words 'Votes for women'.

Gypsy dancer
Make as for the fortune teller, adding a tambourine as follows. Cut a 5 cm (2 in) diameter circle of card and decorate it with a flower design. Glue a 1 cm ($\frac{3}{8}$ in) wide strip of card round the edge of the circle having first cut a few slits in the strip at regular intervals. Glue sequins into the slits, then add a few loops of coloured ribbon.

Country-and-Western singer
Adapt and combine the pop star, cowboy and frontiersman patterns as desired to make this character.

Female pop star
Use the film star for the basic idea, adding the pop star's microphone.

Male show jumper
As for the female, but make the jacket from red felt.

Wizard
Make a long black gown as for Friar Tuck, omitting the collar. Add the cloak and hat as for the witch but omit the hat brim. Sew on cut-out shapes such as moons and stars. Make the hair and beard as for the Viking.

Snow White
Make a doll with bare arms as for the tennis player, with a plain full-length skirt. Add sleeves as for the tennis player making them a little longer and gathering the lower edges to fit the arms. Add a bodice as for the gypsy.

Prince
Make as for Robin Hood using silver or gold trimmings and omitting the hood. Make a cape as for the Viking.

Flower seller
Make the basic doll as for Miss Martha using plain fabrics. Add a shawl as for Cinderella. Make the hair and hat as for the Edwardian lady using plain fabric and trimmings. Fill a tiny basket with bunches of fabric flowers and fix one bunch to the doll's hand.

Schoolboy
Using the desired school colours, make the shirt as

for the cricketer. Make long trousers, or bare legs and short trousers as for the footballer. Add a waist belt. Make the cap as for the cricketer and the socks on bare legs as for the footballer.

Schoolgirl
Using the desired school colours, make the shirt as for the cricketer and a pleated short skirt. Make bare legs, and ankle or knee socks as for the tennis player.

Grandmama
Make the basic doll, skirt and apron as for Miss Martha but bend the doll forward at the waist as for the witch. Add a shawl as for Cinderella. Make the face, hair and hat as for the Fairy Godmother but use a 12 cm (4½ in) wide strip of fabric for the hat and gather it about 2 cm (¾ in) from the lace-trimmed edge. Make spectacles from narrow gold gift-wrapping braid, sewing the braid into a circle for each lens and making an inverted V-shape at the centre between the lenses for the bridge. Give grandmama some knitting, making the needles from 10 cm (4 in) lengths of 3 mm (⅛ in) diameter wooden dowelling. Sharpen one end of the needles and glue beads to the other ends for the knobs. Work a few rows of knitting from a small ball of yarn.

Grandpapa
Make the basic doll with tweed pants and checked shirt, then add a woolly scarf. Make a bald head as for Friar Tuck using grey yarn. Bend the doll forward at the waist as for the witch. Make a waistcoat from felt as for the scarecrow. For a pocket watch, glue a small clock face cut from a magazine illustration on to a small button. Use a bit of gold chain for the watch chain, fixing one end to the watch and the other to the waistcoat front edge. Place the watch in the waistcoat pocket. Add spectacles as for grandmama and a walking stick as for the witch or Edwardian lady.

Edwardian maid servant
Use black fabric and trimmings and make as for the Edwardian lady omitting the shoulder trimmings and the hat. Make a small white lace-trimmed apron, adding shoulder frills and a waistband as for Laura

May. Gather a small frill of lace across the top of the head for a cap. Give the doll a small metal lid for a tray and place a doll-sized cup and saucer on it.

Doctor Whatnot (to go with Hemlock Soames)
Make as for the detective but omit the cape on the the coat, shorten the coat to hip length and add a waist belt made from the same fabric. Make a soft tweedy hat as for the scarecrow and give the doctor a mustache as for the Viking.

Little Bo-Peep
Make the clothes as for the Fairy Godmother using plain fabrics and trimmings. For the crook use a 30 cm (12 in) length cut off a wire coat hanger. Bend the top into a 'crook' shape and tie round a ribbon bow.

Miss Muffet
Make the clothes as for Miss Martha and the hat as for the Fairy Godmother. Give Miss Muffet a doll-sized bowl or plate and a salt spoon. For the spider, gather and stuff a 2.5 cm (1 in) diameter circle of fabric and work four legs on each side with button thread. Work the eyes in small stitches and suspend the spider by a thread from the edge of the hat. For a surprised expression on Miss Muffet's face use the pop star mouth.

Magician
Make the basic doll as for the bridegroom using black felt for the trousers, jacket and top hat. Make the top hat a little taller. Use silky fabric for the waistcoat front, making it from the bridegroom pattern and allowing a little extra on the pattern for turning in the raw edges. Add a bow tie at the neck of the shirt and a mustache as for the chef. Make a black cape as for the witch and line it with red silky fabric. Give the magician a walking stick as for the Edwardian lady or a string of silky scarves appearing from one sleeve.

Mr Snowman
Make the entire basic doll from white fleecy fabric. Add a carrot nose, soft hat and scarf as for the scarecrow. Sew the arms down the sides of the doll, tucking a twig for a walking stick under one arm.

Mrs Snowman

Make as for the snowman with a carrot nose. Add a head scarf, shawl and broom as for Cinderella.

Ballerina

Make the basic doll as for the tennis player using satin fabric and sequin trimmings for the bodice. Make a long or short ballet skirt gathering several long strips of net fabric around the waist. Omit the socks and make the ballet shoes as for the tennis player, binding narrow satin ribbon round the ankles.

Gold prospector

Make the basic doll using worn denim fabric for the pants, checked fabric for the upper body and red fabric for the sleeves. Make another pair of sleeves from checked fabric a little wider than the basic doll sleeves and slip these over the red fabric arms. Sew the tops of the arms and sleeves to the doll, then roll up the checked fabric sleeves to the elbows. Make the hair, beard and mustache as for the Viking. Add a neckerchief, waistcoat and hat as for the cowboy but leave the top of the hat unstuffed, for a well-worn effect. Make a small stuffed bag and tie with thread at the top, and then mark on the word 'GOLD' and sew to the doll's hand.

List of suppliers

Great Britain
Most of the materials can be bought
from local fabric, ironmonger,
handicraft and tobacconist shops
or large department stores, or from
any of the following firms:

Beckfoot Mill
Howden Road
Silsden
Near Keighley
West Yorkshire
BD20 0HA
*For stockinette, felt, fur fabric,
stuffing and other toy-making
accessories.*

Threads and fabrics
Art Needlework Industries Ltd
7 St Michael's Mansions
Ship Street
Oxford

The Felt and Hessian Shop
34 Greville Street
London EC1

Trimmings
Distinctive Trimmings & Co.Ltd
11 Marylebone Lane
London W1

Paper and card
Fred Aldous
The Handicrafts Centre
37 Lever Street
Manchester M60 1UX

Paperchase
216 Tottenham Court Road
London W1

Reeves and Sons Ltd
Lincoln Road
Enfield, Middlesex

Kapok
Woolworth's branches

USA

Threads and fabrics
American Crewel Studio
Box 553 Westfield
New Jersey 07091

American Thread Corporation
90 Park Avenue
New York, NY

Appleton Brothers of London
West Main Road
Little Compton
Rhode Island 02837

Craft Yarns
PO Box 385
Pawtucket
Rhode Island 02862

F J Fawcett Co
129 South Street
Boston Massachusetts 02111

Bucky King Embroideries Unlimited
121 South Drive
Pittsburgh
Pennsylvania 15238

Lily Mills
Shelby
North Carolina 28150

The Needle's Point Studio
7013 Duncraig Court
McLean
Virginia 22101

Yarncrafts Limited
3146 M Street
North West
Washington DC

Paper and card
Grumbacher
460 West 34th Street
New York, NY

The Morilla Company Inc
43 21st Street
Long Island City
New York
and
2866 West 7th Street
Los Angeles
California

Strafford-Reeves Inc
626 Greenwich Street
New York
NY 10014

Winsor and Newton Inc
555 Winsor Drive
Secaucus
New Jersey 07094

Index of characters